ADVANCE PRAISE FOR DEPRESSION: WHAT EVERYONE NEEDS TO KNOW®

"For anyone seeking information about the nature of depression, why it happens, and how it can be assessed and treated, this is your book. Even for those who already know a lot about depression, the comprehensive up-to-date information and the beautiful writing style will make this a bookshelf favorite."
—**Sheri L. Johnson**, PhD, Professor of Psychology,
Director, CALM Program,
University of California Berkeley

"This book is a must-read for anyone interested in and/or affected by depression. Written by a foremost expert on depression theories and treatment, it combines the presentation of cutting-edge knowledge with thoughtful and empathic descriptions of the main symptoms and treatment approaches.

The book not only provides important information, it also offers hope and practical advice to people confronted with the disorder. It should be of great interest to anyone interested in understanding and treating mental disorders."
—**Jutta Joormann**, PhD, Professor of Psychology,
Department of Psychology,
Yale University

DEPRESSION

WHAT EVERYONE NEEDS TO KNOW®

JONATHAN ROTTENBERG

OXFORD
UNIVERSITY PRESS

OXFORD

UNIVERSITY PRESS

Oxford University Press is a department of the University of Oxford.
It furthers the University's objective of excellence in research, scholarship,
and education by publishing worldwide. Oxford is a registered trade mark
of Oxford University Press in the UK and certain other countries.

"What Everyone Needs to Know" is a registered trademark of
Oxford University Press.

Published in the United States of America by Oxford University Press
198 Madison Avenue, New York, NY 10016, United States of America.

© Oxford University Press 2022

Library of Congress Cataloging-in-Publication Data
Names: Rottenberg, Jonathan, author.
Title: Depression : what everyone needs to know / Jonathan Rottenberg.
Description: New York : Oxford University Press, 2022. |
Series: What everyone needs to know | Includes bibliographical
references and index.
Identifiers: LCCN 2020058294 (print) | LCCN 2020058295 (ebook) |
ISBN 9780190083144 (paperback) | ISBN 9780190083151 (hardback) |
ISBN 9780190083175 (epub) | ISBN 9780197586808
Subjects: LCSH: Depression, Mental. | Depression, Mental—
Treatment. | Mood (Psychology)
Classification: LCC RC537 .R6584 2021 (print) | LCC RC537 (ebook) |
DDC 616.85/27—dc23
LC record available at https://lccn.loc.gov/2020058294
LC ebook record available at https://lccn.loc.gov/2020058295

1 3 5 7 9 8 6 4 2

Paperback printed by LSC Communications, United States of America
Hardback printed by Bridgeport National Bindery, Inc.,
United States of America

For Ollie and Cy

CONTENTS

PART II: ORIGINS OF DEPRESSION AND THE DEPRESSION EPIDEMIC

ACKNOWLEDGMENTS

I express my gratitude to Sarah Harrington at Oxford University Press for her care and support with the manuscript. Mary Kleinman helped greatly with research. Members of the Mood and Emotion Laboratory provided early feedback on chapters. Rana Rottenberg provided maternal care and copyediting. Laura Reiley provided nourishment of all kinds.

PART I

DEFINITIONS OF DEPRESSION

1

THE CHALLENGE OF
DEFINING DEPRESSION

What is depression?

A surprisingly difficult question.

Depression has spawned thousands of books. Yet one enduring view is that depression is somehow beyond words (at least when we try to describe the experience). I believe that launching more words (and even another book) about depression is not a futile or vain effort. But let's grant, the subject is full of paradoxes.

Depression is at once intensely private and the most public of problems. People who go through depression are cut off from others, even as they experience symptoms that are shared by millions.

Clinical depression is at once a pressing crisis—the World Health Organization deems it the most burdensome global health problem—and a condition met with shrugs. Despite the severity of the problem and the vast number of people affected, depression garners surprisingly little public mobilization. People don't march against depression or hold golf tournaments or dance marathons to benefit those who suffer.

Another puzzle is that depression exerts the most visible of effects—the many calculable losses tallied by epidemiologists and economists—be it lost work productivity and income, broken marriages, or even deaths by suicide. And yet, at the same time, depression is also invisible and incalculable. There is no test of blood, urine, or genes for depression. Those affected have no obvious stigmata. There is no single telltale sign of the condition.

Then, there is the great imprecision in how people throw around the term depression. Colloquially, the phrase "I'm so depressed" is said as a response to a multitude of everyday disappointments—when rain spoils your picnic, when new couch gets coffee stained, when concert tickets for your favorite band sell out. Such trivial uses of the term depression suggest that depressed people must be whiners and complainers who exaggerate the severity of their problem. Making matters worse, the same term, depression, is also used by clinicians, scientists, and everyday people to mark the most catastrophic of states: when a person is unable to get out of bed, unable to work, unable to self-care, and even consumed by thoughts of suicide. When a single term is used to cover so much territory, widespread confusion about what exactly depression is seems almost inevitable.

So, if we are to cut through the many misunderstandings that surround depression, we need to simplify. Let's begin with its incontrovertible essence: Depression is a kind of mood.

Within us all, we are endowed by evolution with a mood system. This system responds to threats and opportunities in somewhat predictable ways. When we make quick progress toward important life goals, our mood is usually good. When we are blocked in our progress or move away from important life goals, our mood is low. Mood reflects the availability of key resources in the environment, both external (e.g., food, allies, and potential mates) and internal (e.g., fatigue, hormone levels, and adequacy of hydration), and ensures that any animal does not waste precious time and energy on fruitless or even dangerous efforts, such as doing a mating dance when predators are lurking. Given that resources of every sort—be they time, energy, or money—are finite, expending resources on unreachable goals can be ruinous.

The mood system is capable of great variety, from energized highs to everyday blahs to the more severe moods we call clinical depression. The mood system has power over our minds and bodies. Depression is the textbook demonstration of this power. Mood colors our thinking: When we are depressed, thoughts turn to loss, failure, or incapacity. Mood biases our actions: When depressed, we may withdraw, cancel plans, or give up entirely. Mood states even influence our physiology. During depression, the body is aroused, locked in a state of dread—night after night, sleep will be elusive.

The endowment of a capacity for mood inevitably brings with it the potential for both good moods and bad moods, including the unpleasant mood states we call clinical depression. It is likely that virtually everyone has at least some capacity for depression. However, this does not mean that depression is the same for everyone. On the contrary, depression affects different people in different ways. It has many different faces. For some, depression may come out more as a disturbance in thinking; for others, bodily symptoms and motivational changes might be most prominent; for others still, painful emotions are the focal point. Depression may feel wrong or uncomfortable, but there's not a right or a wrong way to be depressed. Depression will likely mean different things to the tycoon on his yacht, the homeless woman living under the bridge, the insurance salesman, or the fashion model, with each appreciating their moods through the prism of their own life history and self-understanding.

Saying depression is a mood and part of a larger mood system orients us. Being oriented is the first step to helping us think more deeply about what depression is and where it comes from. Much complexity remains. As we will see in the coming pages, many different forces act upon the mood system. These include forces we're aware of, such as environmental events, the health of our relationships, our diet, sleep habits, physical activity, light exposure, as well as our own thoughts. But the mood system is also acted upon by unseen forces—forces of which we are not aware—such as the operations of our immune system or stress hormones. Both seen and unseen forces act on the mood system simultaneously. This fact almost guarantees that humans will face a degree of uncertainty about why they are depressed.

This book takes our uncertain posture toward moods as both an assumption and a point of departure for gaining a better understanding of depression. It is natural that the depressed person wonders "Why me?" or "Why now?" and it can be frustrating to individuals or their loved ones when there are no obvious "answers" to these questions. Nevertheless, it is possible to become a more educated consumer of one's own mood, and this book is intended to provide help toward that end. This education includes how to know the difference between depression and normal mood variation; how to better understand the forces that act on mood; and how to better control those forces, including what individuals can do for themselves and how to access additional help from professionals.

How has depression been defined throughout history?

Depression appears as one of the great perils of our times. We read stories about rising rates of depression and commentary that connects it to contemporary trends such as increased use of social media or the ways a gig economy negatively affects workers. The psychological challenges of living amid the COVID-19 pandemic have also fed perceptions that depression is rising in many countries, perhaps to unprecedented levels. Is depression a modern condition?

A glance at history challenges the idea that depression is a malady of the moment. Throughout the centuries, people may have varied in their beliefs about the causes of depression, or what should be done about it, yet the actual descriptions of depression—its key features and how it alters a person's thoughts and behaviors—show remarkable constancy.

Something akin to our modern depression has existed throughout much of recorded history.

Written accounts of a condition similar to what we now know as depression appeared in the second millennium BC in Mesopotamia. One text described when a man had suffered a long spell of misfortune,

> he shakes with fear in his bedroom and his limbs have become weak to an extreme degree; if he is filled with anger against god and king; and if he is sometimes so frightened that he cannot sleep by day or night and constantly sees disturbing dreams; if he is weak [from] not having enough food and drink; and if [in speech] he forgets the word which he is trying to say; then the anger of [his] god and goddess is upon him.

In these writings, depression was discussed as a spiritual rather than a physical problem (one that might be caused by demonic possession). One did not call a doctor; rather, one needed to hail a priest.

The ancient Greeks and Romans recognized melancholia, a condition that again appears akin to modern depression. For example, in *Orestes*, Euripides depicts the tragedy's protagonist hounded by the furies after killing his mother. Orestes' symptoms of depression resemble those of any modern suburbanite: loss of appetite, excess sleeping, lack of motivation to even bathe, constant weeping, chronic exhaustion, and a sense of helplessness.

Greek and Roman authorities on melancholia were split into different camps about its causes. Hippocrates' take on melancholia, or a condition of the "fears and despondencies, if they last a long time," was that it was a biological illness caused by an imbalance in four body fluids called humors: yellow bile, black bile, phlegm, and blood. Specifically, melancholia was attributed to an excess of black bile in the spleen. Hippocrates' treatments of choice to readjust the humors via bloodletting, baths, exercise, and diet. By contrast, Roman philosopher and statesman, Cicero, took another view of melancholia, seeing its roots in psychological events such as rage, fear, and grief. All the while, another great swath of opinion continued to believe that melancholy and other mental disturbances were caused by demons and by the anger of the gods.

In the Middle Ages, Christian religious views dominated European thinking on mental illness. Mental health problems such as depression were largely a sign of God's disfavor, indicating a sinful life and/or a need for repentance. A sea change in thinking came with Robert Burton's 17th-century *Anatomy of Melancholy*. This widely read book offered a variety of explanations of melancholy, including more secular, social, and psychological reasons such as poverty, fear, and loneliness. Burton also included a number of nonreligious recommendations for treating it, such as diet, exercise, travel, purgatives (to clear toxins from the body), bloodletting, herbs, and music therapy. Even if depression cures such as purging or leeches now seem foreign, *Anatomy*'s descriptions of melancholy accord with contemporary psychiatry textbook descriptions of the psychology of the depressed person. Burton lays out an episodic,

> *melancholy* which goes and comes upon every small occasion of sorrow, need, sickness, trouble, fear, grief, passion, or perturbation of the mind, any manner of care, discontent, or thought, which causes anguish, dulness, heaviness and vexation of spirit, any ways opposite to pleasure, mirth, joy, delight, causing forwardness in us, or a dislike.[1]

---

1 Burton, R. (1621[2001]). *The Anatomy of melancholy*. New York: New York Review Books, 143.

In the 20th century, the contemporary term depression gradually came into wider use. Many credit the pioneering 19th-century psychiatrist Emile Kraepelin for increasing the popularity of the word, as well as for the view that depression was due to brain pathology, which remains an important strand in mental health thinking to this day. At the same time, new ideas from Freud and his acolytes viewed depression as resulting from intrapsychic conflict (anger turned inward), a conflict that could be best addressed by talk therapy. To this day, biological perspectives on depression continue to coexist with a variety of psychological and psychosocial perspectives.

The 20th century also ushered in the more standardized diagnosis of depression that currently prevails. As part of a larger effort to handle mental illness similarly to biological diseases, psychologists and psychiatrists put together the first *American Diagnostic and Statistical Manual of Mental Disorders* (DSM) in 1952. In this first manual, which has since gone through several iterations, the term *depressive reaction* was used to describe a condition of severe low mood resulting from an internal conflict or an identifiable event such as job loss or divorce. In the DSM's current incarnation, the principal place where depression is discussed is the syndrome major depressive disorder, which will become familiar later in this book.

Obviously, a Roman soldier, a Greek philosopher, a French peasant, and a New York City cabbie might have very different reasons for becoming depressed. And the authorities of the day would likely offer very different ideas about what each of these persons should do about it, from baths to bloodletting, exorcism, and Prozac. But in another sense, no matter where we turn in history, depression is depression. Each historical personage would likely experience similar symptoms and behave in similar ways, despite the wide gulfs of culture and language between them.

It is important to bear in mind that the evolutionary forces that sculpted our mood system move at a glacial, geologic pace. Evolutionary change is much slower than the pace of human events. Our world of airplanes, computers, and electricity presents us with an unimaginably different physical and psychological environment from what the first *Homo sapiens* faced 300,000 years ago, yet the nervous system that generates mood is basically the same as that of early *H. sapiens*. Because the architecture of our mood system cannot keep up with the furious pace of human events, different historical periods will trigger different amounts of depression in the population (e.g., there is likely more depression in the United States now than in 1950), even as the essential form that depression takes remains the same.

2

THE SYNDROME OF CLINICAL DEPRESSION

What are the symptoms of depression?

Depression is a syndrome. A syndrome is a package of symptoms that group together in a nonrandom way. An example of a syndrome is a strep throat, where the package of symptoms might include a fever, bumps on the tonsils, pain in swallowing, and swollen lymph nodes. In this case, these symptoms package together because streptococcal bacteria have infected the body, prompting a cascade of responses. Confidence that these symptoms signal a genuine syndrome is high: Biological testing can verify the presence of the infectious bacterium as a causative agent.

By contrast, the syndrome of depression is not based on objective tests. Instead, it rests largely on observation of symptoms and on accumulated clinical wisdom. A variety of clinicians and researchers have noticed over time that certain psychological complaints are packaged together. Patients who complain of a low mood, for example, also tend to complain of fatigue and sleep difficulty. When enough of these symptoms co-occur, they can be diagnosed as the full depression syndrome, which is also called a *major depressive episode*. Ultimately, a depression diagnosis is founded on a careful assessment of a patient's symptoms—piecing together what the patient says, as well as how the patient is behaving. Although a clinician can filter or interpret the information provided by the patient, it is ultimately the patient's report of symptoms that grounds a diagnosis rather than the state of their blood or brain.

So what *are* the symptoms of depression? I illustrate the nine symptoms of depression with the case of Lonnie, a 24-year-old freelance writer who has become depressed after the breakup of a long-distance relationship. Full disclosure: Lonnie is not a single identifiable depressed person. Like other cases presented in this book, she is a composite, sketched from the many interviews with depressed people I have conducted over the course of my research studies.

Cardinal symptoms

Two symptoms are considered so characteristic of depression that one or both are required for diagnosis:

  A sad, low mood that the person can't shake: Lonnie describes her mood as "hollow." Most days during the past 3 months, she has felt empty or gloomy most of the time. Occasionally, her mood brightens for an hour or two, sometimes for no obvious reason. Unfortunately, these lighter periods don't last.

  A loss of interest or pleasure in things the person usually enjoys (which goes by the technical term anhedonia), which can apply to hobbies, friends, or sexual relations: Lonnie loves fashion and her professional writing covers the fashion industry, but since she has become depressed, she doesn't open any of the glossy magazines or mail-order catalogues that she receives; these pile up un-read on her coffee table. Her best girlfriends call her to make a date, hoping to cheer her up; she declines. Normally extroverted, Lonnie prefers now to keep to herself.

Associated symptoms

In addition to the cardinal symptoms, there are seven other associated symptoms of depression. A person must have at least five of the nine symptoms in total to be diagnosed:

Sleep problems: Sleep problems can manifest as an inability to fall asleep or stay asleep. The opposite pattern, sleeping much more than usual, is another possibility, but it is not as common. Lonnie's case evidences classic insomnia: Every night she falls asleep like a ton of bricks only to wake up around 3 a.m., 4 hours before her alarm. Instead of falling back to sleep, she lies in bed ruminating on her failures, on what went wrong in her relationship, dreading the coming of the next day.

Problems with mental focus: This can appear as concentration problems or as an inability to make decisions. Lonnie struggles with her writing. She also detects that her mind is not working right when she finds herself in the grocery isle, paralyzed in front of a display, unable to choose which kind of sandwich bag to buy.

Changes in weight or appetite: The depressed person most typically will lose weight and eat less (due to depression, not an intentionally planned diet). Sometimes, depression can bring about the reverse pattern of increased weight or appetite. Lonnie had this symptom in a dramatic fashion. Previously a gourmet cook who loved food, she has dropped two sizes during the past 3 months and has to force herself to eat, often skipping meals. When asked about her appetite, she says, "These days I want to eat about as much as I want to clean the toilets."

Fatigue or loss of energy: Depressed people typically state that they feel tired most or all of the time. Lonnie continually feels run-down. She has to rally herself to perform the most routine of tasks, such as taking her poodle for a walk around the neighborhood. She describes this tired feeling as like "the worst ever hangover," without the fun of a party the night before.

Pathological guilt: The depressed person is often wracked by pervasive guilt about things that they have done or not done. Depressed people often come to doubt their fundamental worth as a person. Lonnie feels guilty for "being born"; in her mind, she continually goes over the ways she has been a terrible friend and a lousy daughter. She is haunted by the thought, "I am a waste of space."

Psychomotor changes: Most typically, the depressed person talks or moves more slowly than normal. Some depressed people show the reverse pattern of agitation and restlessness. With Lonnie, her family and her therapist both notice that her speech is slowed; when she talks on the phone, her voice is a monotone; when asked a question, there are inexplicably long pauses before she responds.

Suicidality: Suicidality is the most frightening of depression's symptoms. The depressed person may have general thoughts about the topic of death or specific thoughts of hurting themselves, which can lead to planning or attempting suicide. Lonnie's case this manifests as a "passive death wish"—as she drives on a two-lane highway, she wonders if it might be better if the oncoming car swerved in front of her.

Other common features

In addition to the previously discussed nine official symptoms, there are other behaviors that are also highly characteristic of depressed persons. Although they do not make the diagnostic manual as part of the recognized syndrome, they are very much worth noting:

Anxiety: Anxiety is like depression's shadow. Most depressed people report elevated levels of anxiety. Lonnie is constantly on edge; her muscles feel tense; she worries constantly that she won't get better and that she will lose her job and all of her savings.

Self-focused thinking: One of the most characteristic things depressed people do is to focus on themselves. Lonnie spends extended periods each day in solitary thought trying to understand why she is depressed; she keeps a journal in which she tracks her mood hour-by-hour and tries to connect any mood change to her activities and sleep. She dwells on her failings; she returns again and again to the idea that god or some unseen power might be punishing her by keeping her depressed.

Pessimism: Depressed people believe that the future will be worse than the present; it is a great struggle for them to maintain any degree of hope. Lonnie doubts that her antidepressant medications will be able to make her better; she doubts that she will be strong enough to survive her depression if it continues another 6 months. She is essentially one giant doubt. In her worst moments, she thinks to herself, "My life is over."

Unexplained aches and pains: Depressed people commonly report physical complaints such as headaches, back pain, aching muscles, and stomach pain. One odd thing Lonnie noticed before she was diagnosed with depression was a pain on the left side of her chest; she worried something might be wrong with her heart, even though she was an athletic person in her 20s. After a medical workup, her family doctor could find no explanation for her chest pain complaint. Ultimately, this pain complaint would just be attributed to the depression, as yet another mysterious element of the condition.

Irritability: Depressed people often feel agitated, restless, and short-tempered. Lonnie has days where everything and everyone gets on her nerves. Sometimes she gets so charged up that she struggles to find a safe outlet for her furious rage; she is angry with her family, angry with her ex-boyfriend, angry with her dog, angry with the entire situation. She doesn't scream and yell at those who have wronged her. She mostly holds it in, her main release going to her bedroom and punching into her pillows.

Self-medicating: Depressed people often struggle so much with their moods that they are (understandably) tempted to abuse substances to control them. Self-medication goes far beyond how patients might take liberties with their antidepressant drug prescriptions. It includes a variety of other substances—chemicals that might be used to drown out pain or take the edge off anxiety. This includes drinking alcohol excessively, abusing opiates or sleep medications, or becoming addicted to anti-anxiety drugs such as Valium. For her part, Lonnie has become dependent on her sleep medications. Her pill stash is her dirty little secret. She is always experimenting with it; she hopes that if she takes the right amount of the drug at the right time, she will be able to sleep through the night. But this seldom happens; she instead ends up with the worst case—poor quality sleep and feeling woozy the next day, slowed down by the aftereffects of the sleep medicine.

How is clinical depression different from a sad mood?

Clinical depression is diagnosed when patients report at least five of nine of the official symptoms of a major depressive episode and when these symptoms are experienced for at least 2 consecutive weeks. Unfortunately, Lonnie is well in excess of these thresholds. However, we should recognize that the five of nine symptoms threshold for clinical depression is somewhat arbitrary. Arbitrary boundaries are common in many diagnostic thresholds—for example, the exact number at which "high blood pressure" begins is more a convention than demarking a specific boundary of a disease.

The boundary for defining clinical depression, although important for guiding decisions, should not be considered completely absolute. Many people have troubling depression symptoms that fall short of the threshold for diagnosis. Imagine Chuck, who recently reports three depression symptoms: He has lost interest in activities, can't sleep, and is experiencing constant fatigue. These symptoms cause him distress and hinder his work as a school principal. In clinical practice, people such as Chuck who have "subthreshold" symptoms of depression might be monitored for any worsening of their condition or they might be treated immediately, depending on the clinical judgment of the practitioner. Milder forms of depression are common, simply because all forms of depression are very common.

The existence of these milder forms of depression raises a larger question: How exactly is clinical depression different from "ordinary misery" or even a garden-variety sad mood?

In a key way, clinical depression is not different in kind from an ordinary sad mood. Clinical depression and ordinary sad moods are both products of the same mood system. Factors such as environmental stress or not getting enough sleep that render a person more vulnerable to clinical depression are the very same factors that render a person vulnerable to a garden-variety sad mood. From this perspective, the difference between clinical depression and an ordinary sad mood is just a matter of degree.

Even if it is made from the same building blocks as a sad mood, clinical depression can feel different to the sufferer. For one, clinical depression is stronger than a sad mood. States of clinical depression may be experienced as completely overwhelming. Clinical depression also lasts longer. Research that tries to map the typical duration of these states bears this out. Fortunately, ordinary sad mood will typically last hours or days. By contrast, the criteria for a major depressive disorder require a minimum 2-week duration, and typically, clinical depression lasts much longer, 4–6 months. The greater strength and duration of a clinical depression have real-world consequences for sufferers. As Lonnie's mood deepened and as she could not stop it, she became ever more fixated on why she was feeling so bad and why she couldn't shake it—a self-sustaining cycle that further deepens her mood.

This underscores another potentially important difference, one that Lonnie notices, also typical of people who struggle with clinical depression: Clinical depression is more difficult to cope with than ordinary sad mood. When she experiences a normal sad mood, Lonnie can think of a dozen or more things she can do to cheer herself up, at least for a while. Watching her favorite show, eating a good meal, spending an evening with her girlfriends, spending half an hour at the gym, and even sometimes just taking a quick nap can all leave her feeling somewhat restored. By contrast, during her clinical depression, nothing she does seems to reliably lift her mood. For the past 3 months, Lonnie's mood has basically been a brick wall, explaining her deep frustration, her loss of hope, and why she has become obsessed with every tiny fluctuation in her mood.

The distinct human experience of clinical depression is important to acknowledge: People who struggle with clinical depression often report that it "feels different" from an ordinary sad mood. This explains why people throughout history have perceived clinical depression in a strange and even frightening state. Lonnie, like many patients, says it's difficult for her to put her finger on exactly what's different, partly because it is so difficult to describe moods. She says that during her depression, rather than actually feeling sad, she feels "numb and cut off from my feelings, like I have an urge to cry but can't."

Finally, clinical depression, in part because it is stronger and lasts longer than ordinary sadness, creates far more impairment than ordinary sadness. A clinical depression can infer with people's ability toto work, go to school, take care of their children, or maintain their relationships. In severe cases, the depressed person may be bedridden or fail to maintain personal hygiene. For Lonnie, the most notable impairment caused by her clinical depression was her inability to write. Normally, she could knock out a freelance assignment in a day or two. Her depression slowed her thinking and her writing to the point that just sitting at the keyboard and pecking out a few sentences became a struggle. She wanted to take a break from freelancing, but she had clients that were expecting finished stories and, frankly, she needed the money. This impairment also took an emotional toll: As deadlines came and went, Lonnie felt she was fundamentally incompetent, that no one would ever hire her again, and that no one ever *should*. Her case fundamentally illustrates how the different symptoms of depression can cascade and built upon one another.

How does clinical depression range in its severity?

To the previous point, we have been discussing how mood ranges from ordinary sadness to clinical depression. However, even after we cross the threshold into clinical depression, there is still considerable range left to cover. Clinical depression itself varies in its severity.

Patients with severe depression have typically well over five depression symptoms, and their symptoms are intense and impairing. For example, a patient with severe anhedonia may derive zero pleasure from any activity and be unable to conceive of anything that would give them pleasure in the future. Common patterns in severe depression include substantial weight loss and staying in bed for substantial periods of time because of a lack of motivation or energy. Typically, severe depression features dramatic alterations in a person's behavior. Even basic hygiene such as showering, brushing teeth, or putting on clean clothing may be compromised. Likewise, in severe depression, cognition can be disturbed to the point of an outright break from reality. For example, a person's feelings of guilt may be transformed into an unshakeable psychotic belief that the person is the devil. By contrast, in milder depression, a person may feel distress and may demonstrate more subtle alterations in cognitions and behaviors. At the same time, a person with mild depression may be able to function normally in many areas and may be concealing the symptoms from others for weeks or months at a time. In fact, people with milder depression may find that the condition subsides before they recognize a need for treatment or before they get help.

Perhaps not surprisingly, extensive research demonstrates that severity of symptoms is an important basic characteristic of depression. Generally speaking, more severe depressions are more challenging to treat; they tend to last longer than mild or moderate depressions and are more likely to recur.

What is the difference between unipolar depression and bipolar disorder?

In discussing depression, this book focuses on unipolar depression, the more common group of the mood disorders. The *uni* in unipolar depression is what it sounds like. People with unipolar depression have one set of problems; these problems lie exclusively at the low pole of mood, encompassing the sorts of depression symptoms we have been discussing.

By contrast, people with bipolar disorder have problems at the high pole of mood. The high pole in bipolar disorder involves periods of what are called hypomania or mania; these are mood episodes in which people experience abnormally elevated or euphoric or sometimes irritable mood, along with associated symptoms such as racing thoughts and a tendency to pursue dangerous or risky activities. Although it may sound like fun to have abnormally elevated moods, the highs of bipolar disorder can be quite destructive, with people spending their life savings, abusing drugs, and making other poor life choices.

People with bipolar disorder most typically have two sets of mood problems. In addition to problems at the high pole of mood, periods of depression, at the low pole of mood, are also characteristic. Bipolar disorder can be particularly treacherous to cope with, as a person oscillates between the plunging lows of depression and the soaring highs of mania or hypomania. Signs of this difficulty, the classic forms of bipolar disorder, are associated with both high rates of hospitalization and high rates of attempted and completed suicide.

Bipolar mood disorders are different from unipolar depression in a number of other ways. First, the psychology differs. Because bipolar disorder also involves abnormal highs, it can be even more of a confusing roller coaster than unipolar depression, both for the person directly affected and for the person's family. Treatments for bipolar mood disorders also differ. Most important, a class of drugs called mood stabilizers, the best known of which is lithium, are used to try to even out the highs and lows of bipolar disorder. In fact, many in psychiatry express concern that traditional antidepressants can aggravate or worsen mood instability in a person who has a bipolar mood disorder. Some researchers also believe that bipolar disorders are more strongly controlled by genetic risk than are unipolar mood disorders. Because of these many differences, diagnostic systems such as the *Diagnostic and Statistical Manual of Mental Disorders*, fifth edition, traditionally separate depressive disorders and bipolar mood disorders in different sections. For these reasons, our knowledge about unipolar depression may not apply well to bipolar disorders. Specific resources for persons with bipolar mood disorders are included in the Resources section.

3

WHEN SHOULD I WORRY THAT I MIGHT BE DEPRESSED?

Case Study: Jose

What's wrong with me? Five months ago, Jose asked that primal question. The first odd thing he noticed was being as weak as a kitten—just walking up a flight of stairs left him totally drained. Not only was Jose tired and run down, his thinking was fuzzy. Reading a policy memo, he kept going over the same paragraph. He felt unwell. Was it the flu, he wondered, or could it be depression?

At first, he discounted the possibility. Did he really have reason to be depressed? Yes, he was often harried at his job as a health policy analyst, but other things in his life were going just fine. He had a mostly good marriage; he owned his own home. He was fortunate to have close friends. Turning 50 maybe stirred some midlife anxiety, but his health to this point had been okay. His feelings didn't totally compute. How *could I be depressed when most of my life was going okay*? As the weeks rolled on, he decided, "It's just job stress." It was more comfortable to believe depression was a label that didn't apply to him.

But the feelings didn't pass. After 2 months of further struggle, Jose decided he had to see a doctor to get to the bottom of his symptoms. He emerged from the appointment with a diagnosis of depression and a slip of paper with a name of a drug scribbled on it. A week into the medication, he was waiting for the pills to work their magic.

Depression doesn't always trumpet its presence when it visits a person. This is in part because there's no bright line between the ordinary "blahs" and the syndrome of clinical depression. So, when is it reasonable to worry that you or your loved one may be facing the serious possibility of clinical depression? Here are some clues:

Strong and durable symptoms: As noted in Chapter 2, clinical depression is stronger and lasts longer than ordinary sadness. Although ordinary sadness can move one to tears, depression more fully takes over the body and mind. For example, Jose felt physically weakened, and he was not able to focus his attention on his work. Likewise, experiencing a low mood for a day or a week, with or without a reason, is consistent with ordinary mood variation. Jose's low mood went on for months relatively uninterrupted—a worrisome pattern. Depression has an insistence and a persistence to it that ordinary sadness does not.

Difficulties functioning: Depression involves a more significant change in functioning than does ordinary sadness. Usually when people are sad, they can still do their work, relate to others, and take care of life's mundane business. It is reasonable to worry about clinical depression if mood impairs any of these major life domains. In Jose's case, he now struggled to write the policy memos that usually came so easily for him. He started to avoid his friends and acquaintances, and he stopped exercising, previously a joy and an outlet.

Feelings are out of scale with the situation: Another warning sign that something more than simple sadness may be afoot is when environmental events cannot explain the depths of the person's feelings. It's natural to have a period of sadness after being snubbed by a friend or when your favorite sports team loses a title. Major losses such as the death of a close family member will trigger more significant depressed mood (including the possibility of clinical levels of depression). In Jose's case, he discounted the possibility that he could be depressed because there were no clear events that could explain his feelings. That's actually a misconception because clinical depression does not *require a trigger*. In fact, careful studies of life events demonstrate that many people who are diagnosed with depression do not report any obvious trigger event beforehand.

The possibility of clinical depression is, understandably, unsettling or frightening for many. Some are scared by the associations of a diagnosis: Could it mean you are a "crazy person" who has "lost their mind"? Others, unfortunately, continue to hold the outdated view that a mental health diagnosis signifies a personal failing. Still others recoil from diagnosis because they are afraid of contact with the mental health system ("I'll be given medications against my will or put in a straitjacket"). Such attitudes explain why Jose—like many people—may want to attribute depression symptoms to something such as run-of-the-mill job stress. Fear of diagnosis and a reluctance to enter treatment may help explain why surveys find that more than half of people who meet diagnostic criteria for depression do not use treatment services. Jose's case also illustrates another way depression is often undertreated: Even when people enter treatment, that entry comes only after a lag—after depression has run unchecked.

Can I self-diagnose?

If you've read to this point, you've learned about the symptoms of depression. As a book-reading, savvy person, you're likely to also know that there are tests you can take on the internet that profess to reveal whether a person has depression. You may wonder: Why even go to a treatment professional? Why not just take a free test and self-diagnose?

You certainly can self-diagnose, and for people who have had extensive experience with depression (i.e., many previous episodes), self-diagnosis might be reliable. For everyone else, a self-diagnosis of depression is error prone and may provide a seriously incomplete picture.

A segment of depression self-diagnoses will be false-positive errors (making a diagnosis when it is not merited). False-positive errors occur because sometimes things are, in reality, not as bad as they seem in our minds. Some people are temperamentally anxious or are just prone to see the worst in themselves, leading to an exaggerated report of symptoms. For such individuals, a clinician's careful, independent assessment of symptoms may reveal that the concerned person is well short of a depression diagnosis. In such cases, a professional's assessment may provide some reassurance. If treatment for depression is not yet indicated, contingency plans can be made in case symptoms worsen.

Self-diagnoses of depression can also produce false-negative errors (missing a diagnosis that is present). Some people (like Jose) may be motivated to mask the true severity of their symptoms; denial of our problems is a common human foible. At other times, people miss symptoms because they lack knowledge about depression or because they lack self-insight. In all such cases, the value of a careful, thorough, independent clinical assessment is that it corrects for such biases and can discover the reality of a diagnosable depression, even when this is not what the person "wants to hear."

The errors of self-diagnosis are often magnified by the self-tests that are used. In the past 20 years, the information that had exploded on the internet is akin to a new Wild West. Self-tests on depression, and on other mental health conditions, have proliferated with virtually no regulation. Consequently, it is easy to "click" on many depression tests or screenings on the internet and be blissfully unaware that the questions you are answering are not from a validated instrument. Of course, use a poor test and erroneous results are more likely. Fortunately, some self-tests do use validated instruments. For example, when the search term "depression" was used on Google, U.S. users were directed to a depression test in the top group of results, and the search engine commendably used the Patient Health Questionnaire-9 (PHQ-9)—a short instrument that has at least demonstrated prior validity. A published study showed that if you have a high score on the PHQ-9, odds are fairly good that a clinician would independently find you to be diagnosable with depression. Even with the best of these self tests, however, we are straining their purpose by asking them to provide a "yes" or "no" answer on diagnosis. Remember that these tests were originally intended to be used for screening, not as stand-alone tests to render a diagnosis of depression by themselves.

I make these points not to denigrate people's curiosity about themselves or to discourage people from visiting credible health-oriented websites that are geared for the consumer (e.g., WebMD and Healthline). Indeed, these websites often present solid information about depression, and using such resources is beneficial when it helps people become more informed about the condition or find appropriate treatment resources. But the trend toward self-diagnosis, in part fueled by such websites, also has a dark side. For example, self-diagnosis may paradoxically play into treatment avoidance. As more people hold an unsupported view that information on the internet is sufficient to manage or even cure depression, many may not wish to consult with professionals at all, even when they experience severe symptoms. The reluctance to seek professional support may explain why it is so common for people to experiment on themselves with home remedies for depression that are unproven and untested.

What are better ways to diagnose depression?

If self-diagnosis is less than ideal, what procedures should be used to diagnose depression?

In diagnosing depression, self-report questionnaires or self-tests can be used as a starting place. But it is critical that such measures are then incorporated into a more comprehensive assessment that is performed by a clinician. The clinician is valuable for several reasons.

One source of value is that a well-trained clinician almost surely has more experience than you do in assessing the symptoms of depression. One challenge for a patient is that their symptoms typically fluctuate. For example, you might perceive at different moments during the week that you are more motivated or less motivated—so how should you answer a general question about motivation? A good clinician will ask questions about different activities and contexts that help provide a better overall sense of the symptom. Another challenge in assessing your symptoms is that you are just you, with just a single point of reference. By contrast, the clinician has seen hundreds or even thousands of previous patients, which helps provide a better yardstick for judging the true clinical severity of, for example, your loss of motivation. For certain populations, the clinician perspective is even more essential. Perhaps most notably, depression is more challenging to diagnose in children and adolescents; the symptoms can appear somewhat different in children, and young people often have difficulty reporting on their problems.

In addition, a good clinician—by virtue of their training—can place the depression symptoms in a wider explanatory context. For example, the clinician can evaluate the possible role of drugs or medical conditions in contributing to depression. The clinician can distinguish depression from the symptoms of related conditions such as an anxiety disorder. For example, a good clinician will take a careful history to assess whether a depressed person has a history of bipolar mood episodes (mania or hypomania), which is critical because the treatment for persons with bipolar disorder is often different than the treatment for persons with unipolar mood disorders. This brings us to the last point: Formal diagnosis by a trained clinician adds value over self-diagnosis because it accelerates the process of getting matched to an appropriate treatment.

All this said, let's consider three better ways of diagnosing depression. We can grade them by their strength, calling them bronze, silver, and gold standards:

> *Bronze standard*: Use of a valid depression self-test in con-junction with a brief clinician encounter. In reality, most depression is diagnosed this way, in primary care settings. Advantages here are that the physicians will have some training in depression and also will almost certainly have prior clinical experience with depression because it is one of the most commonly encountered conditions in primary care. The disadvantages are that most office encounters in primary care—especially in the United States—are quite brief, which permits only a hasty assessment. In addition, family doctors or pediatricians have less extensive training in mental health than do specialists. Very often, however, when depression is se-vere or complex, a general doctor will refer such cases to specialists in psychiatry or clinical psychology.
>
> *Silver standard*: Use of a valid depression self-test in con-junction with a detailed psychiatric assessment. The best assessments are semistructured diagnostic interviews that last 1 or 2 hours and take a full history of a person's mental health problems, including depression. This type of interview is usually carried out by a mental health professional such as a psychologist or psychiatrist.
>
> *Gold standard*: The ideal way to diagnose depression is three pronged—the valid depression self-test, the detailed psy-chiatric assessment, and an evaluation of physical health (assuming no such health examination has taken place

recently). Such an evaluation may involve a physical examination, blood tests, and other follow-up, as needed. An assessment of physical health is advantageous because several conditions might cause or contribute to depression, including infections, neurological diseases such as dementia, and metabolic disease. For example, some people are depressed because of low levels of thyroid hormone, a finding that would suggest the value of exploring a distinct treatment pathway, namely thyroid replacement. Alternatively, if a person is found to be in good physical health, the lack of problems can help rule out obvious medical explanations of the depression.

4

THE PREVALENCE
OF DEPRESSION

How common is depression?

Depression is a very common problem—so common, it has been dubbed "the common cold" of psychiatry. Indeed, mood disorders are the most common reason for psychiatric hospitalization. Under the premise that you cannot tackle a problem until you can accurately describe it, this chapter presents a basic aspect of depression—its prevalence.

At any given moment, between 2% and 4% of the population is depressed. The World Health Organization's large World Mental Health surveys have found that over a 1-year interval, nearly 6% of people will have depression. Prevalence expands further when we consider depression over an entire lifetime; one of the most trustworthy estimates of lifetime depression derives from the National Comorbidity Study Replication, which found that almost 17% of the U.S. population had the condition. When considering estimates of lifetime depression, it is important to bear in mind that some people who have not yet experienced depression will develop it later. Conservatively, a fair estimate is that approximately 20% of the population in Western industrialized countries—one in five people—will develop depression during the life course. Estimates of depression from non-Western and non-industrialized countries are fewer; although prevalence rates are sometimes lower in non-Western contexts, depression appears to be a common mental health problem nearly everywhere.

Simple prevalence numbers do not fully convey the burden of depression. For one, depression episodes often recur. Half of people who have one episode of depression will have one or more recurrences. Episodes of depression can also be long-lasting. Although episodes of depression last on average approximately 6 months, some people experience chronic depression that can last years. The fact that depression is often recurrent, and sometimes chronic, helps account for why approximately half of people who have lifetime depression will experience an episode of it during any given year.

Is the prevalence of depression increasing?

It appears that the prevalence of depression is rising, but the case is not entirely straightforward. One challenge is that we don't have hard estimates of depression from earlier points in human history. There are certainly no believable estimates of depression from the periods of the Renaissance, French Revolution, or even the Great Depression. Credible estimates using stable criteria for what we call depression begin in the second half of the 20th century.

Even now, it is no mean feat to accurately gauge the prevalence of depression in the population. There is always some degree of error when depression is measured. Both the person gathering the data and the person reporting on their depression are subject to pitfalls: Memories fail, questions are posed in unclear ways or are misunderstood, or interviewers misinterpret the ensuing responses. Another source of potential error in estimating depression derives from the difficulty of obtaining a fully representative sample of, for example, a nation. Sampling problems can interfere with obtaining precise estimates on simple questions, such as those regarding voting preferences. Most people are aware of the periodic flops of political polling. Rest assured that all population estimates of depression contain some degree of imprecision.

However, multiple sources point toward an increased prevalence of depression in the late 20th and early 21st century. These include the following:

- A 2018 Blue Cross study based on 41 million health records showed a large increase in depression diagnoses from 2013 to 2016.
- Numerous studies indicate a disturbing cohort effect with depression. Specifically, in a number of countries, depression is increasing among younger generations of people, tending to strike at earlier ages, especially in the teen years.
- Consistent with this cohort effect, the National Comorbidity Survey, based on a sample of 200,000, found that the incidence of major depressive episodes in adolescents had increased significantly between 2005 and 2014, increasing from 9% to 11%.
- Depression appears particularly rampant in university populations. A 2012 survey of U.S. college students by the American College Health Association found that 33% of women and 27% of men identified a period in the previous year of feeling so depressed that they had difficulty functioning. A similar 2019 survey of 68,000 students found that 20% of students were diagnosed with or treated for depression in the prior year. This trend is not restricted to the United States. For example, a 2017 UK study found that 94% of institutions reported increases in demand for mental health services, with depression the most common mental health problem among students. This situation on campus is not likely to ease anytime soon: A July 2020 survey of 18,000 college students found that 80% of students reported worsening mental health as a result of the COVID-19 pandemic.
- Data from 607,520 respondents to the National Survey on Drug Use and Health (an annual U.S. study of persons aged

12 years or older) revealed that the prevalence of past-year depression increased significantly among U.S. persons from 6.6% in 2005 to 7.3% in 2015. Notably, the rise was most rapid among those aged 12–17 years, increasing from 8.7% in 2005 to 12.7% in 2015.

- There are also concerning increases in behaviors linked to depression, most notably in deaths by suicide. In 2018, the U.S. Centers for Disease Control and Prevention (CDC) released data on suicide from 2000 to 2016 based on cause of death from death certificates. These data revealed a nearly 30% increase in the suicide rate during this period. Although depression is not the only factor that contributes to increases in suicide, it is one of the main factors.

- In 2011, the CDC reported that antidepressant use in the United States increased nearly 400% in the past two decades, making antidepressants the most frequently used class of medications by Americans aged 18–44 years.

- Evidence points to a broader pattern of deteriorating mental health in the population. For example, in the United States, the tally of those who were so disabled by mental disorders that they qualified for Supplemental Security Income or Social Security Disability Insurance increased nearly two and a half times between 1987 and 2007—from 1 in 184 Americans to 1 in 76.

- Globally, according to a World Health Organization report released in 2017, the total estimated number of people living with depression increased by 18.4% between 2005 and 2015 to a staggering 322 million. The increase came both from global population growth and spikes in depression in particular age groups.

These statistics may seem overwhelming and to leave no room for doubt. Yet several important voices have questioned the existence of a true depression epidemic. Allan Horwitz and Jerome Wakefield argue the underlying reality of depression has changed little during the past few decades. What has changed, they contend, are perceptions about depression. If ordinary people become more sensitive in labeling bad feelings as abnormal and doctors likewise become more sensitive, we could expect a growing number of people who seek treatment for depression and an increase of diagnoses and prescriptions for antidepressant medications. Relatedly, psychiatrist Allen Frances has warned that clinicians have become increasingly "liberal" or loose in how they diagnose depression. In this view, diagnostic overreach is pathologizing increasingly more of ordinary sadness and people's responses to garden-variety stress as clinical depression.

Another related idea is that culture can be an echo chamber to perpetuate depression. Greater awareness and sensitivity about depression could fuel more dialogue about depression in popular culture, including more articles about depression in the media and more scientific literature on the topic. There could be a sort of vicious cycle in which increased dialogue about depression leads to more labeling of life's problems as depression, whether that dialogue comes from mental health advocates trying to fight its stigma or pharmaceutical companies that have a financial interest in people being diagnosed with depression.

In addition, changes in how people use technology could also be playing into the statistics. Ready access to the internet has made it easier for people to search and find information about depression, and there is evidence that the more people seek information about depression, the more they might tend to self-diagnose.

It is challenging to subject the skeptics' ideas to a conclusive proof. We have gathered some of the compelling evidence for a depression epidemic. However, not all data point to an increase in depression over time. In fact, several of the most carefully performed longitudinal studies conflict in their results. Some studies do find increased prevalence of depression. But other studies that used the standardized diagnostic criteria in multiple waves of assessment conflict find no change in depression prevalence rates in several countries, including Canada and the United States. In summary, there is broad evidence of a depression epidemic, but sound science also requires that we keep an open mind until the matter is completely settled.

A depression epidemic? Sorting out the evidence

How can we reconcile conflicting claims about a depression epidemic? One response is that that these claims may not be as conflicting as they first appear to be. There likely is a real increase in the phenomenon of depression; that real increase is reflected in the hard statistics of disability filings and insurance claims, as well as in overwhelmed counseling centers and, most tragically, suicide. At the same time, the epidemic skeptics may be correct that some of the increase reflects changes in how depression is reported. There may be less hesitation now than in past decades for people to seek help, as well as less resistance than previously to label life's problems as depression (especially among the young). Thus, what we may have in depression is both the reality of a depression epidemic and an epidemic that is being inflated by cultural trends, such as changes in how depression is noticed or discussed. In the following chapters, we consider some of the reasons why this already common disorder may be increasing.

5

THE CONSEQUENCES OF DEPRESSION

How does depression impact mental and physical health, relationships, and careers?

Depression is obviously painful and distressing, and for those reasons alone, we want to curtail its sway. But there are numerous other serious harms associated with depression that also warrant attention.

In yet another demonstration of how the mind and body are connected, depression has been linked to a wide array of physical health problems. In epidemiological studies, depression is consistently associated with cardiac problems, arthritis, asthma, cancer, diabetes, and chronic pain. Depression is associated not only with insomnia but also with other sleep disorders, such as obstructive sleep apnea. Consistent evidence of the connections between depression and ill-health naturally spawns research designed to determine what explains these connections.

One intuitive proposition is that depression might be a consequence of ill-health. Simply stated, ill-health is upsetting. Indeed, there is evidence that the experience of illness and the stress of being sick can feed feelings of depression. Even learning about a serious health problem can be difficult to cope with and, for some people, be enough to bring about a depression.

At the same time, there is also evidence for the reverse idea—that depression can precede and even possibly cause a host of other health problems. Some of the most compelling data derive from the study of cardiovascular disease. People who have episodes of depression are more likely to have a first onset of coronary artery disease, including incidents of heart attack and stroke. Studies have shown that in patients with established heart disease, bouts of depression make the course of their disease worse, including a greater risk for subsequent heart attacks and premature death. These findings, in turn, raise further questions about why depression may have harmful effects on internal organs such as the heart. How can such ill effects be explained?

Research shines a light on some of the ways that depression might harm the body. For example, a state of depression might increase the amount of stress hormones that are circulating in the body, which in turn may reduce immune functioning and make people more susceptible to infection. Another strand of research has linked depression's harms to increases in the body's inflammatory response. Inflammation accompanies depression for reasons we do not yet completely understand. Importantly, chronic elevations of chemicals involved in the inflammation process have been linked to a number of diseases, such as diabetes, arthritis, and heart disease.

Depression may also impair health for a simpler reason: Depression makes people behave in unhealthy ways. For example, depressed people may eat and sleep poorly; may be more likely to abuse alcohol and other substances; and may be less likely to adhere to advice from a doctor, including not taking their medications as directed.

Research on the connections between depression and ill-health is ongoing. But the question is not an academic one. The toll that depression takes on health is very real. This toll is reflected in the most sobering fact of all: Depression predicts an elevated risk of death, even apart from death by suicide.

In addition to exacting harm on the body, depression also strains relationships, sometimes to the breaking point. A person who is struggling with depression can often be difficult to interact with; the person can be interpersonally withdrawn, irritable, and needy. These are interpersonal patterns that can strain families, friendships, and romantic relationships. Depressed persons report smaller networks of supportive persons and that their relationships are of a lower quality. For instance, studies of marriage have found that when a partner has more depressive symptoms, more discord and dissatisfaction prevail in the relationship.

Interpersonal patterns in depression can feed a vicious cycle: Not only does being in a bad relationship tend to make people more depressed but also depression tends to erode the quality of relationships over time. In a marital relationship, the occurrence of depression before a marriage predicts subsequent divorce, including higher divorce rates even after a depressed person has recovered. Interestingly, there is evidence that some of the marital harms of depression can be undone. For instance, when couples engage in marital therapy, not only can there be an improvement in relationship quality but also depression symptoms in both people can decrease.

Unfortunately, depression appears to have adverse effects on the family. For example, when parents struggle with depression, it is more difficult for them to parent effectively, and there is more likely to be high levels of family conflict, including parent–child conflict. Some of the family consequences of depression even cross generations. Depression in a parent, in turn, predicts more behavioral problems developing in a child, and these behavioral problems do not necessarily abate after the parent's depression subsides. There is even documentation that depression in a parent, particularly a mother, increases the chance that a child will go on to develop depression. Although part of the increased risk for depression in biological offspring comes via genetic inheritance, genes are not the whole story, and researchers have pointed to problematic interpersonal processes as one of the major culprits.

Depression also adversely affects people's educational attainment and career trajectory. Depression has been associated with interruption of education, such as high school or college drop out. For those who remain in school, grades and other metrics of achievement may suffer because depression can disrupt concentration and motivation. On the job, people who struggle with depression tend to have lower productivity. They are more likely to be absent from work and underperform when they are present. Economists have tried to calculate the total economic toll of depression, and this tally is a challenge, given depression's high prevalence and wide impacts, including on job performance. One credible estimate is that depression costs the U.S. economy $210 billion annually. These costs are not only collective, but individual: people who struggle with depression are more likely to lose their jobs.

Most studies that examine the consequences of depression evaluate what happens over the short term. A smaller body of work documents adverse long-lasting effects of depression. For example, children who develop depression are more likely to have depression and other mental health problems in adulthood. One landmark study by Myrna Weissman and colleagues found that when a cohort of adolescents who had depression were followed into adulthood, 10–15 years later, they had increased occurrence of psychiatric and medical hospitalization, as well as impaired functioning in work, social, and family life relative to their peers.

Reviewing the broad array of depression-related consequences helps us understand why depression creates so much disability. Depression is prevalent and it is often recurrent. People who have a history of depression regularly struggle with the symptoms of depression, and having the symptoms of depression can impair a person's functioning across a number of roles. In fact, when depression was compared to other health conditions in 24 different countries, it was associated with greater role impairment than nearly all other physical health conditions and all mental health conditions. This is because depression often sets in motion a kind of chain reaction. We might think of Lonnie (introduced in Chapter 2), who can't concentrate when depressed, who then develops financial problems because she can't finish her writing assignments, which makes her stress hormones sky-rocket, which reduces her immune function, which leads her to catch a bad case of the flu, which worsens her mood, which sets her productivity back further, and so on.

Which mental health problems usually co-occur with depression?

Perhaps the strongest illustration of depression cascading with other problems is the domain of mental health. Here, depression often occurs together with other mental health disorders, a phenomenon called comorbidity. Studies of diagnostic patterns in community samples (and in clinical samples) document that comorbidity between major depressive disorder and other mental health conditions is more the rule than the exception.

One of the most extensive studies of comorbidity is the National Comorbidity Study–Replication. That investigation and others like it have reinforced the idea that depression does not occur in insoluation but presents alongside other mental health problems. Nearly three out of four people who have depression will experience another mental health condition in their lifetime. Often, the other mental health problems will be active at the same time as the depression, complicating treatment and coping efforts. The following are mental health problems that most commonly co-occur with depression:

Anxiety disorders: More than half of depressed persons will have a lifetime anxiety disorder, such as phobias, social anxiety disorder, or panic disorder. Anxiety disorders appear to have the tightest connection to depression relative to any other mental health condition. Interestingly, longitudinal studies often find that an anxiety disorder will precede the emergence of clinically significant depression.

Trauma and stress-related disorders: Depression is commonly observed among people who have been exposed to a major trauma. Depression is also extremely common among people who have been diagnosed with post-traumatic stress disorder.

Substance use disorders: Roughly one-fourth of depressed people will have substance use problems. As you might expect, the relationship between the two conditions is often mutually reinforcing. Many people abuse substances to cope with depression; this is sometimes called the self-medication hypothesis. In turn, the chronic use and abuse of substances can precipitate or worsen depression, in part through the ways that substance use can disturb brain functioning.

Psychotic disorders: Depression is common in people who have schizophrenia. In addition, some presentations of depression blend together mood problems and the typical symptoms of psychosis, such as hallucinations and delusions. One such presentation is called schizoaffective disorder.

Eating disorders: Eating disorders such as anorexia nervosa, a condition in which a person refuses to maintain their body weight, are also common among depressed people. Eating disorders and depression overlap in part because both disorders become more prevalent in adolescence, particularly among females. Again, there is evidence of a mutually reinforcing relationship. For example, an adolescent girl may develop an eating disorder in response to chronic feelings of depression, especially the poor self-image. In turn, depression can also be a consequence of the eating disorder, including physiological changes that are set in motion by self-starvation.

Comorbid diagnoses present additional challenges for people struggling with depression. People who present with multiple simultaneous mental and physical health issues generally fare more poorly over time and are more difficult to treat compared to people who present with depression alone.

Why does depression so often co-occur with other mental health problems?

One of the major questions in depression research is why depression so often clusters with other mental health problems. Several reasons explain comorbidity. Some proposed reasons are simple. As mentioned previously, the other problems might cause depression, or depression might cause the other problems.

But other explanations for comorbidity are more subtle. For example, depression might cluster with another mental health problem because it shares a common environmental cause. Events such as losing one's job, divorce, or having a serious health problem are likely to activate both feelings of anxiety and feelings of depression. Likewise, traumatic events such as sexual or physical abuse may be the common wellspring for post-traumatic stress disorder and depression.

Sometimes depression clusters with other mental health problems because there are shared or overlapping risk factors. For example, there may be genetic characteristics that increase risk for substance disorders and these same characteristics also increase risk for depression. Likewise, there may be personality predispositions, including a trait called neuroticism (a tendency to experience negative emotions, particularly under stress), that are linked both with depression and with many of its comorbid mental health diagnoses.

Incidentally, a contingent of scientists, such as Thomas Insel, views the high overlap of risk factors and the high degree of diagnostic comorbidity as signaling that there is something seriously wrong with the entire *Diagnostic and Statistical*

Manual of Mental Disorders (DSM) diagnostic system. The observation that people routinely qualify for three, four, or five mental disorders, according to these critics, tells us that there are more diagnoses in the DSM than there are true mental conditions. According to these critics, diagnoses that look different based on their surface symptoms, such as depression and generalized anxiety disorder, might essentially be alternate forms of the same condition, due to their high degree of overlapping risk factors. The critics argue that the message of comorbidity is that the DSM needs to be radically overhauled. Whether additional research leads to revisions to future editions of the DSM, including how depression is diagnosed, or to adoption of entirely a different diagnostic system remains to be determined.

Although it is sobering to review the wide array of depression-related harms, there are also hopeful developments to consider. One exciting idea connected to common pathways or risk factors is that it might be possible to treat several mental health problems simultaneously. In a sense, this is already observed with some depression treatments. For example, antidepressant medications such as selective serotonin reuptake inhibitors are often helpful not only in reducing the symptoms of depression but also for treating several anxiety disorders, as well as some eating disorders. This is also observed with psychotherapy: Scientists such as David Barlow have been attempting to develop "unified protocols" for treating multiple emotional disorders at the same time with one psychotherapy procedure. That medication or psychologically based treatments can be further optimized to better address comorbid mental health problems is an exciting prospect.

Does depression ever have any positive consequences?

The conventional wisdom is that depression invariably has destructive and cumulative effects that compound over time.

Obviously, most of the demonstrated consequences of depression are negative, including severe consequences such as premature death. Given the awful nature of some of these harms, a research focus on the negative consequences of depression makes sense. Still, is it possible that depression sometimes has a silver lining?

Research in other areas of psychology supports the idea that depression can hold benefits for some people. For example, research on trauma has documented that some take the experience of a negative event in positive directions: Finding benefit in adversity can become an ongoing source of strength. Similarly, proponents of evolutionary perspectives, such as Paul Andrews, have argued explicitly that depression can provoke successful adaptation under certain circumstances. One key idea is that depression may be a mechanism that forces people to focus their attention on a complex life problem; this obsessive processing on the negative, although painful, may help people ultimately solve the life problem. As Randolph Nesse notes, the features of depression "can prevent calamity, even while they perpetuate misery."[1]

The idea that depression might have benefits is not just a theory. Some experimental data show ways that a low mood might confer benefits to thinking and decision-making. For instance, there are clues that depressed persons are better at detecting deception in others and can sometimes be more realistic in their thinking than are nondepressed people. Work on the possible benefits of depression remains in its infancy, a hypothesis in need of testing.

Intriguingly, some formerly depressed people also report that the experience of depression helped them become more resilient. Indeed, one theme in narratives of depression

---

1 Nesse, R. M. (2000). Is depression an adaptation? *Archives of general psychiatry*, 57(1), 14–20.

survival, including those of celebrities such as Dwayne "The Rock" Johnson, is that episodes can act as a true rock bottom, meaning a person's worst-point experiences could ironically offer a foundation or support for subsequent positive life change. Later in this book, I explore the idea that for some, depression could represent a turning point—a hinge where people move toward greater well-being via rediscovered purpose in life, cultivation of new strengths, forging a new career, or leaving a toxic relationship behind.

PART II

DEPRESSION

PART II

ORIGINS OF DEPRESSION AND THE DEPRESSION EPIDEMIC

6

BIOLOGICAL CONTRIBUTIONS TO DEPRESSION

Is depression a "chemical imbalance"?

You've likely heard the analogy: Depression is like diabetes, a "chemical imbalance." The chemical most often mentioned as imbalanced is a neurotransmitter—a chemical messenger in the brain—called serotonin, which is hypothesized to be low in depressed people. Although serotonin gets the spotlight, fellow neurotransmitters dopamine and norepinephrine are also mentioned in the conversation.

If we follow the analogy, like the diabetic person who needs insulin, the depressed person needs a drug such as Prozac to correct their imbalance and restore serotonin to normal levels. The idea of a correctible chemical imbalance is popular with the media, mental health professionals, and patient advocate groups. Pharmaceutical companies heavily promoted the "chemical imbalance" idea in their direct-to-consumer advertising throughout the 1980s and 1990s. Through sheer repetition, the idea has become popular. For example, a 2007 survey of undergraduate students found nearly 85% believed it was "likely" that chemical imbalances cause depression.

The widespread use of serotonergic drugs [selective serotonin reuptake inhibitors (SSRIs)] for treating depression has further boosted the serotonin theory of depression. But just as headaches are not caused by a lack of aspirin, the efficacy of serotonergic drugs does not prove that depression is caused by a lack of serotonin. Although the idea of a chemical imbalance in depression is intuitively appealing, the reality is far more complex.

In fact, after studying this question for more than 50 years, neuroscientists have struggled to support the core of the theory and demonstrate that serotonin is low in depressed people. Part of the problem is that it is very difficult to estimate levels of serotonin, or any neurotransmitter, in a live human's brain. Researchers have used several different measurement methods to get an approximate idea, without obtaining clear and replicable results. Currently, no reliable tests are available to determine if you have a chemical imbalance in your brain; chemical imbalance is not used in the diagnosis of depression, nor do health professionals monitor the state of said imbalance during depression treatment. Unlike insulin and diabetes, which can be tested and closely monitored during treatment, chemical imbalances have surprisingly little direct practical significance in the management of depression.

An additional problem with the chemical imbalance theory is that antidepressant drugs alter neurotransmitter levels very quickly yet the drugs typically take weeks to work—a lag that does not jibe with the theory. Then, there is the obvious: The actual efficacy of the antidepressant drugs is less than over-whelming; they do not work at all for approximately one out of three patients. All of the previously mentioned problems suggest a simple version of the chemical imbalance is, at best, seriously incomplete.

With time, more data have amassed that present other serious hurdles for the low serotonin theory of depression. These include findings reported in the flagship journal, *Archives of General Psychiatry*, that indicate increased serotonin activity in depressed persons. In addition, a newly developed antidepressant drug (Tianeptine) is believed to *decrease* levels of serotonin at synapses. Growing evidence suggests that it may be an error to even talk about the brain having a single serotonin level.

Based on work with rats and mice, neuroscientists are increasingly moving to the view that there are different populations of serotonin neurons that are each independently regulated.

In summary, although neurotransmitters surely are important players in the communication system of the brain and likely play some role in mood, and although it stands to reason that serotonin, dopamine, and norepinephrine might be altered by depression, science does not offer a crisp formulation of exactly how these chemicals are altered. Antidepressants continue to be used clinically, but there is no single tidy theory that explains why they work when they work. As chemical imbalance theories have flagged, neuroscientists have become more interested in testing more complex ideas, such as depression involving dysfunction in wider brain circuits or pathways.

If someone asks you, "Isn't depression a chemical imbalance?" you can say, "It's not so simple. Despite what you might have heard, there isn't evidence for a single chemical imbalance." It is important to try to set the record straight. Despite the weakness of the science, public presentations of depression-as-diabetes continue unabated, with Prozac and the other SSRIs starring as insulin. The chemical imbalance theory of depression is exhibit A for the gap between science knowledge and public discourse.

Is depression due to bad genes?

It is well known that depression runs in families. For example, offspring of a depressed parent(s) are two or three times more likely to develop depression (and other mental health problems). Differences in the family environment may explain part of this. For instance, a depressed parent can hurt family dynamics. A depressed person's parenting is more often harsh and likely to enflame conflict. But another reason why depression runs in families may have to do with the shared genetic endowment among relatives—a concept called heritability.

Research has provided tantalizing clues that genes explain part of the familial risk for depression. Twin studies track to what extent we can predict depression risk as a function of genetic similarity. One key comparison is between identical twins (100% genetic similarity) and fraternal twins (50% genetic similarity). If genes are the story of depression, identical twins should be much more similar in their depression level than are fraternal twins. Twin studies find that to be true, allowing us to put numbers to the question of heritability. Their conclusion is that approximately 30–40% of risk for depression flows from generic variation.

Adoption studies potentially offer powerful demonstrations of heritability because they provide a method for studying the environmental effect, disentangled from the genetic influences of having a depressed parent. Parent–child adoption designs typically compare genetic risk conferred by biological parents who were not involved in rearing their children and the environmental risk conferred by adoptive, rearing parents. Adoption studies have demonstrated that both genes and environment matter. Both the rearing environment and the genetic contribution from the biological parents can influence depression in adopted children.

These studies tell us a big fact about depression: Genetic variations are one of the major routes to it. But at this point, the research hit major roadblocks. We can't go much further than repeating the big fact. Yes, genetic variations explain substantial amounts of depression risk but we still don't know which genes are implicated, nor what the putative bad genes might be doing to make depression more likely.

One problem that scientists have run up against is that depression is polygenic—meaning that many genes are involved. After exhaustive study of the genetic material of hundreds of thousands of persons, the search for a single gene responsible for depression has been called off. There is no white whale. As a polygenic condition, a large number of genetic variants are involved in the pathway to depression; each genetic variant exerts only a tiny effect in the pathway, with no variant necessary or sufficient to cause depression.

The situation with depression sharply contrasts with a single gene disorder, in which a single genetic variant confers all the risk. With single gene disorders, such as Huntington's disease, it is far easier to identify the bad gene and what the genetic variant does in the body. It is also easier to develop genetic tests for the condition and possibly even correct the faulty gene. All of these tasks are far more difficult for polygenic disorders.

Ultimately, "the big fact" is difficult to use. Not only are there many problem genetic variants in depression but also these variants interact or combine with one another in unpredictable ways; given the vast number of possible combinations, it becomes even more challenging to zero in or isolate the sources of genetic risk. Finally, another complexity is that genetic vulnerabilities for depression may lie dormant until they are activated by another factor. For example, a person with genetic vulnerability may not be liable to develop depression unless the person encounters environment adversity. This kind of complexity—known as a gene–environment interaction—also makes it more difficult to act on our knowledge of genes.

In summary, the story of genetic risk for depression is one of "so close but yet so far way." Over and over, we see that "bad genes" explain a component of risk for depression, but over and over researchers, clinicians, and patients are blocked from acting on this information. There is no accepted genetic test for depression, nor any type of gene therapy available to the consumer. In the future, it may be possible to use a person's genetic profile to determine what type of drug or psychologically based treatment might be especially helpful for treating their depression. Currently, however, this kind of personalized treatment work is aspirational. Current solutions are low tech: If you know depression runs in your family, be mindful that you and your relatives are all at elevated risk for developing depression, and be vigilant for depression's warning signs.

What has research on the brain taught us about depression?

Let's take it as a given that the brain implements all mental functions, moods, and actions (there is no real alternative). Thus, it is a reasonable assumption that depression involves the brain in some way. But how? Impressive new technologies now allow scientists to probe the brain in great detail. These technologies include functional magnetic resonance imaging (fMRI) and positron emission tomography, which permit detailed studies of the brain in action. During the past 20 years, these technologies have received massive investments, including of money, time, and expertise. As a result, there are now thousands of research studies on the brain and depression. What have we learned?

Research has produced many findings about the brain and depression, but, as yet, there is no smoking gun. Arguably, there is no gun.

Brain imaging studies have revealed, for example, that certain brain areas differ in size between depressed and mentally healthy individuals. Studies of brain structure attempt to compare the size of different brain areas between depressed and nondepressed people. For example, the amygdala, which responds to the emotional significance of events, tends to be smaller in depressed people than in those without the disorder. Other brain centers that appear to be reduced in volume are the hippocampus, an interior brain region involved in emotional memory; the anterior cingulate cortex, which helps govern impulse control and empathy; and certain sections of the prefrontal cortex, which plays an important role in planning and the regulation of emotions.

It is important to underscore that these findings are correlational. Yes, depressed and nondepressed people show differences in brain structures. It is uncertain whether these differences are a cause of depression. Are they instead an effect of depression? Or do these brain differences reflect the operation of some other factor, such as exposure to drugs? In other words, we have some initial findings of brain differences, but the meaning of these differences remains unclear. One interesting possibility is that some of these results could reflect depressed persons' exposure to a prolonged stress response, working from the idea that sustained elevations in stress hormones inhibit brain growth. (This explanation has also raised interest in developing drugs to block elements of the stress response as potential therapies.) Finally, however intriguing, it is important to remember that these results just tell us about an average tendency of depressed people. Lonnie is more likely to have a smaller amygdala—but a smaller amygdala is not guaranteed. Lonnie may well have a normal-looking amygdala. Indeed, many healthy subjects have amygdalae that are reduced in size. These results are not diagnostic: One cannot look to a brain scan to determine whether or not a person has depression.

Another set of studies have focused on trying to compare the degree of activity in different brain areas between depressed and nondepressed persons. Functional neuroimaging studies using fMRI have revealed that the anterior cingulate cortex is often less active in depressed people and that the amygdala can be less active or more active, depending on the study. Some parts of the prefrontal cortex also tend to show diminished activity. Like findings in brain structure, these findings with functional imaging are correlational and reflect average tendencies. It is again uncertain whether differences in brain activity tell us about the cause of depression, the effects of depression, or the effect of some other factor that is connected to depression (e.g., poor diet or environmental stress).

Research using brain scans continues to be published in great volume. New findings from brain imaging research on depression are regularly trumpeted on television and the internet, complete with striking graphics such as color-coded brains, creating the impression that the cause of depression has been discovered in the brain; problem solved. Unfortunately, journalists often omit the qualifying details; the scientists are happy to have the media coverage and may not include all appropriate caveats. Without knowing the qualifiers or the fine print, the public is left with the false impression that depression has divulged its secrets to neuroscience.

Just as with genetics, when the simple ideas didn't work out, neuroscientists moved toward more complex hypotheses. There is now less investment in the idea that the structure or function of individual brain areas will provide the key to depression. Instead, there is more focus on patterns of connectivity or connections between different brain areas. For example, Helen Mayberg and colleagues have been investigating the hypothesis that depression involves abnormal connections between structures of the prefrontal cortex and limbic structures, emotional centers, deeper in the brain. (The full details are not important here, but the core concept is that depression disturbs the normal reciprocal relationship between decreased metabolism in the prefrontal cortex and increased metabolism in limbic regions.) These studies of brain connectivity continue to produce intriguing results; it is too soon to evaluate whether this harvest will have a greater yield than previous approaches.

So there are reasons both to like and to dislike brain research on depression. Or to feel ambivalent about it. On the plus side, a database of descriptive findings has accumulated about the brain and depression. Description is a first step toward deeper understanding. Although these findings do not have much utility for mental health professionals or for patients, in the future this knowledge could form the building blocks for breakthroughs. There is also continuing potential for improved therapeutics coming directly out of brain research. A good example is transcranial magnetic stimulation, a noninvasive technique that involves inducing an electric current within the brain using pulsating magnetic fields that are generated outside the brain near the scalp. This technique, which is approved in the United States for treatment-resistant depression, has shown some initial promise and may be refined with time.

On the minus side, it is questionable whether the massive investment in neuroscience research over the past 20 years have paid off. So far, we do not have even a single discovery that could be considered game changing for the understanding or treatment of depression. Interestingly, at the same time that public health authorities in the United States and Europe have prioritized research on the brain for funding, pharmaceutical companies have pulled back on their drug development research by as much as 70%, suggesting that the field is running into dead ends. From this perspective, it is fair to ask whether costly brain-based depression research should continue to be a top priority for public funding, and especially as we face a world of constrained resources.

7

ENVIRONMENTAL AND PSYCHOLOGICAL CONTRIBUTIONS TO DEPRESSION

Is depression the result of stress?

Stress seems ubiquitous in today's distraction-filled world of deadlines, conflict, and noise. Four of five Americans say they are afflicted by stress sometime during the day. Across the globe, the COVID-19 pandemic has ramped up perceptions of stress, contributing to health worries, financial stress, as well as family stress. Stress is a common term in everyday parlance. In fact, like depression, the concept of stress has lost specific meaning with its constant repetition. In fact, many people use "stressed" and "depressed" as interchangeable terms.

What's the relation between stress and depression? To better understand the role of stress in depression, researchers have focused on the idea of a major or severe life event. Examples of severe events include being diagnosed with a serious illness, the breakup of a marriage, or being fired from one's job. These sorts of severe events have been found to be harbingers of depression. In fact, more than half of depressed people report a severe stressor before the onset of their episode. Interestingly, everyday hassles and minor stressors appear to have a weaker relationship to episodes of depression than do severe stressors. For depression, exposure to one major stressor is more impactful than exposure to many smaller aggravations.

A stress–depression connection makes sense from the perspective of the mood system. Our mood system is tasked with continually tracking environmental opportunities and threats. When we feel in over our heads—when we face major challenges without adequate resources—our perceptions of stress soar. When does stress become depression? There is no hard and fast rule, but specific types of threats are more likely to push people over the line, such as when stressors are intense, have a long-term impact, and especially when a person is left feeling trapped or humiliated.

Imani was pushed well over that line. Her marriage had gone sour in recent years, and she had been considering divorce. Two weeks after she engaged in a brief infidelity, she learned her husband was dying of cancer. She felt guilty for the affair, and somehow, she even felt guilty for the cancer. Even as Imani continued to feel that her marriage was not worth saving, she could also not leave her dying husband. As her depression spiraled, Imani was the picture of a person trapped in a bad situation, as both leaving her husband and staying with him as he died seemed like utterly untenable options.

One caveat, even the nastiest major stress does not push everyone into an episode of depression. In fact, only approximately one-fourth of people who face major stressors become clinically depressed. This mirrors the variability seen with more garden-variety stressors. For example, when their airline flight gets canceled, some travelers are placid, others are livid, and still others are anxious. People facing major life stressors also diverge in their trajectory. For Imani, major stress led to depression; for others, stress can trigger substance use problems; for still others, the consequences of stress might be schizophrenia or anxiety disorders. And there is the group of envied souls who face down the hardest situations while retaining good mental health.

Stress only sometimes leads to depression. Again, this illustrates that there's no single recipe for depression. Research on stress also suggests that recipes for depression are complex and usually combine several ingredients, like a stew. Stress, for instance, is more likely to lead to depression when a person has a weak support network, engages in negative thinking, or has a biologically based vulnerability to depression, such as predisposing genes.

Another strong clue that stress is not the full story of depression is that many episodes of depression occur in the absence of any obvious stressor. Think of Jose, who erroneously believed he couldn't possibly be depressed because his life was going okay. Stress is an ingredient for depression, but it is by no means a necessary ingredient.

The bottom line is that major life stress has an important relationship to depression. At the same time, important areas of mystery remain. Why do some people become depressed after exposure to major stress, whereas others do not? Why do some people get depressed repeatedly without any exposure to major stress? Should mental health professionals treat stress-related depressions any differently than non-stress-related depressions?

Does depression stem from negative thoughts?

Philosophers have argued for centuries about whether an objective reality exists, which may ultimately be unanswerable. In the meantime, psychologists have demonstrated the many ways that our reality is shaped by how we think about it. This is the process of cognition, which includes what we pay attention to, how we draw conclusions, and what we remember. There is no question that the ways that people think influence how they feel and what they deem important.

When in therapy, Shelia is asked about her day. She says the traffic was horrible and that work was boring; she does not mention all the compliments she received on her new outfit or that her medical examination revealed no health problems. Clinicians and researchers have long noticed that many depressed people are like Shelia. When asked about virtually any topic, their responses tend to be pervasively negative. It is as if the depressed person sees the world through black-colored glasses.

For decades, psychiatrist Aaron Beck has been one of the most astute observers of depressed persons' thinking. He noted a pattern he dubbed the cognitive triad, which covers three broad areas of negative thinking:

- Negative thoughts about the self: Shelia says, "I'm stupid. I'm unattractive."
- Negative thoughts about the present. Shelia observes, "I have no real friends" and "I hate my supervisor."
- Negative thoughts about the future: Shelia wonders, "Why do I bother? I'm going to die alone."

Can Shelia's negative thoughts by themselves cause depression? Not necessarily. Although many people who hold negative thoughts do become depressed, many others with similar thoughts do not. In other cases, negative thoughts can be a consequence of depression rather than a cause of it. So how does negative thinking contribute to depression?

As with stress, negative thinking appears to combine with other factors to make depression more likely. In fact, a pattern of negative thinking may be what helps life stress turn into depression. A habit of negative thinking may also be important in explaining why a few symptoms of depression might worsen and become a full-blown depression episode. One negative thinking pattern that has been of keen interest is called *rumination*, which is when people think obsessively about their sadness, such as what might be causing it or why they can't stop it. Research finds that people who engage in this sort of obsessive rumination about sadness are more likely to struggle with more long-lasting depression compared to people who distract themselves from their sad mood.

One important clue that negative thoughts help sustain depression is what happens when the negative thoughts are curtailed. An important type of therapy, cognitive–behavioral therapy (CBT), is explicitly designed to interrupt negative thinking patterns. CBT is one of the leading treatments for depression. For many, it serves to shorten episodes of depression; over the long term, CBT may help people ward off depression's return. Although there may be several reasons why CBT is effective, its efficacy suggests that developing skills to control negative thinking has considerable value in combatting depression.

Why, then, do people engage in negative thinking if it paves the way to misery and depression? There are likely several reasons. First, people do not always recognize that they are engaging in negative thinking. Shelia, for example, is convinced that she sees the world realistically. When she says everyone at work is against her, she does not seem to be aware that she is exaggerating her colleagues' slights and criticisms and failing to notice her bosses' supportive statements. It is difficult to become aware of our thought processes because our thought processes often run automatically, in the background. When people are in a very low mood, negative thinking is effortless (just like when you are at a funeral and sad memories come easily); because negative thoughts are so automatic for depressed people, friends and family should try to be patient and avoid blame when a depressed person becomes mired in them.

In addition, people often do not recognize the connections between their negative thinking and their depression. For example, Lonnie engages in obsessive rumination about why she is sad because she believes it helps her gain insight into her problems, even as the habit of fixating on her mood leads her to feel worse. Finally, negative thinking may also be part of a larger human tendency toward self-defeating behaviors—wrecking a diet with a binge of fattening food, returning to a drug habit when it costs family support, or staying with an abusive spouse. In this way, negative thinking may be a self-defeating aspect of depression. Lonnie knows her pessimism is over the top, yet she still allows herself to be governed by it, such as when her cash reserves are dangerously low yet she doesn't apply for freelance writing work because she's sure she won't be selected.

Negative thinking is no doubt an important aspect of depression. Still, key questions remain for researchers. Where exactly does negative thinking come from? To what extent does it reflect an inherited temperament? To what extent might negative thinking grow out of difficult life experiences, including those of childhood? As people recover from depression, to what extent do their patterns of negative thinking go away and to what extent do they remain?

Does depression stem from relationship problems?

Humans are social animals. Given our social needs, relationship problems make us vulnerable to depression. Threats to relationships—whether the relationship with a close friend, a marriage or life partner, or a family member—or terminations of relationships by breakup or death are major triggers for depressed mood. Indeed, this follows a key function of our mood system—to carefully track the status and health of our relationships.

Relationship problems also illustrate how readily different ingredients of depression combine together. Major life stress often prompts depression. When we examine which life events are the most stressful, it is remarkable how often such events feature a serious problem in a close relationship. Likewise, negative thinking may be a liability for depression, but when we take a closer look, we find that much our negative thinking revolves around relationships. In this, Lonnie is fairly typical. Her recent breakup with her boyfriend is a prompt to rehearse her failings; she starts by reviewing all the mistakes she made with Jack; soon she's replaying everything from childhood onward that she's ever done wrong.

There is often a vicious circle at work with depression and relationships. Relationship problems help set depression in motion and, in turn, depression makes relationship problems worse. Here, as elsewhere, there's the question of which is the chicken and which is the egg. In this case, it seems clear that relationship problems can be both an effect of depression and a cause of it.

It is important to note that interpersonal problems aren't like lightning bolts that strike down the unknowing. People often do things (both wittingly and unwittingly) that bring about successive rounds of relationship problems. Psychologist Constance Hammen has conducted extensive research on the concept of stress generation, which focuses on ways that people create the interpersonal chaos that leaves them depressed. Among the problematic patterns are the following:

Poor relationship choices: Imani has low self-esteem, yet she keeps gravitating toward men who put her down, which locks in her poor self-image, creates friction-filled relationships, and leads her to feel chronically depressed.

Constantly seeking reassurance: Joe constantly expresses insecurity and a need for reassurance about himself and his ongoing relationship. Initially, his girlfriend goes along with it, but after a while she finds his requests exhausting. Eventually, she leaves him, just as his friends and previous girlfriends have done in the past.

Excessive valuation of relationships: Kristen's self-worth is completely bound up in her relationships. She tends to be clingy and submissive, and she fears rejection. She believes that without a man, she is nothing. Her depression gets triggered nearly every time a relationship dissolves, yet she feels compelled to rush into a new one to fill the vacuum. Interestingly, this relationship style is more common in females than males. Some commentators believe excessive reliance on relationships partially explains why adult females are more likely than males to have depression.

Although these examples highlight romantic and friend relations, stress generation can apply as easily to difficulties in other interaction contexts, such as with co-workers, roommates, or family members. The more interpersonal stress the depressed person generates, the more other people seem like land mines. It is no wonder that people with depression wind up feeling chronically misunderstood, unloved, and fearful of interactions.

From another perspective, family and friends might find it frustrating to interact with a depressed person. That's understandable. At the same time, persevering for a loved one can make a major difference for his or her depression. Considerable data show that when depressed people have robust support from their social networks, they are more likely to get through their episodes quickly and be more able to cope with stress.

Interestingly, therapies that improve relationships and relationship skills often greatly benefit depressed people (the benefits of marital therapy were previously mentioned). Perhaps most notable is interpersonal psychotherapy (IPT), one of the best supported of all depression treatments. IPT is a form of psychotherapy that attempts to help people better navigate relationship problems by helping them with social role transitions (e.g., retirement and moving to a new city), managing grief, building social skills such as assertiveness, and improving communication in interpersonal disputes. The clear efficacy of IPT for depression further cements the idea that relationships are one key to understanding depression.

Yes, relationship problems are a major trigger for depression, and depression-prone people often behave in ways that make the situation worse. However, there is more we need to know: What are the key factors that explain why some people become depressed after relationship problems, whereas others do not? What explains why people repeatedly make interpersonal choices that play into depression, and why is it so difficult for them to learn from prior experience? When people repeatedly create relationship stress for themselves, what is the best way to break that cycle? How can we help people choose and maintain more constructive relationships?

Can depression result from childhood events?

What happens early in life can reverberate far into the future. Even the first moments of a fetus gestating in a mother's womb can impact childhood and adult development. For example, the researchers of Project Ice Storm found that the extent to which mothers were stressed in early to mid-pregnancy predicted psychological and behavioral problems in their offspring at age 11 years.

Let's unpack this a little. How could gestational events in a mother increase the chance of their future offspring's depression more than a decade later? One key possibility involves maternal stress, which might directly or indirectly help create a harmful biological environment for the developing child. This could happen if the mother secretes elevated stress hormones that pass through the placenta to the fetus and, in turn, fetal exposure to these hormones subsequently impairs development, including aspects of the brain. Another possibility is that expectant mothers might try to cope with stress by smoking more cigarettes or using other drugs; increased substance use may adversely affect the environment of the womb. Finally, anxiety in the mother may reduce blood flow to the fetus. Reduced blood flow is a risk factor for premature birth and low birthweight, which are both associated with future depression.

For anyone about to become a mother (or a father), the idea that gestational events could push their child toward depression is a little terrifying. It's also a little puzzling. There is such a vast gulf between a tiny embryo and an adolescent or young adult experiencing that first bout of depression. How might we think of a chain of events to connect them?

An analogy might help. Imagine depression is like a fire in a factory. After the factory fire, safety inspectors are asked to go to the scene to determine the cause. The inspectors find that there was a short caused by faulty wiring that led to a spark that happened to fall on a pile of oily rags, igniting the rags. Because the sprinklers on that floor were not working properly, a small rag fire soon engulfed the whole factory. What was the cause, then? Was it the bad electrical system? The spark? The rags? The faulty sprinklers? Or none of these things? In the end, the inspectors report that all of these events were needed to come together to make the fire. In fact, it would seem that the fire was far from inevitable, and it could have been averted at several points along the way. If we think of depression in this way, adverse childhood events might be like faulty wiring or oily rags—not inevitable causes of depression but events that elevate a risk of depression over time.

After a child is born, a wide variety of experiences and events have been demonstrated as potentially increasing the risk of later depression. Not surprisingly, problematic rearing conditions are among them. Being raised by parents who are harsh or neglectful, being raised in an institution such as an orphanage, or losing a parent to an early death all increase subsequent risks for depression. Arguably, the most heartbreaking events that increase future depression risk for children are physical and sexual abuse. Physical abuse may alter youth psychology in important ways, leading to lower self-esteem, difficulties interacting with peers, and even an increase a biologically based vulnerability to depression.

We are still learning all the reasons why traumatic events have the potential to increase risk for depression years or even decades later. Trauma can even alter aspects of our biology previously thought to be fixed. The field of epigenetics, which blurs the line between nature and nurture, has discovered that certain experiences have the ability to change genes, specifically altering whether or not particular genes are expressed. Stress is among the factors demonstrated to affect epigenetic processes such as DNA methylation (when methyl groups are added to part of the DNA molecule and can prevent certain genes from being expressed). Changes to gene expression after stress may explain how exposure to a trauma in childhood could lead to an enduring depression vulnerability, and such a process may even explain why those who were stressed in childhood have more difficulty coping with stress in adulthood.

Children are not passive victims of adversity. It is easy to overlook how youth actively attempt to cope with horrible situations. When children act in ways that upset teachers, parents, or peers, it is easy to label the behaviors as pathological and not see ways that their behaviors might be understandable reactions to trauma and serve the children in other ways.

Imagine Jasmine, a 10-year-old girl raised by emotionally distant parents who are unaware as a trusted neighbor molests her. Jasmine may be confused by the experience and have no one to tell. She may well be blamed or disbelieved by her parents, or she may be frightened about what might happen to the neighbor if she speaks up. In such a scenario, chronic feelings of anxiety and sadness are natural. What should Jasmine make of a world in which primary attachment figures—parents—are emotionally unavailable and unable to help when a trusted neighbor turns into an attacker? Her mood system, like the mood system generally, is forward looking. It assumes that if the worst has already happened, it can and will happen again. Best to be prepared. Given the shocks that she has already been exposed to, it makes sense if Jasmine is given to anxious moods scanning for danger (especially in relationships); it makes sense that Jasmine is given to sad moods during which she analyzes her mistakes and missteps. These behaviors are her last lines of defense against further ruin. Like a suit of armor that provides protection from slings and arrows, Jasmine's guardedness is also a heavy burden to haul around.

In considering childhood adversity and depression, there is an unfortunate imbalance between research on risk and resilience. Research on risk—what sparks the fires of depression—has been emphasized much more than resilience—how children cope and how the flames of risk are averted or extinguished. This imbalance is unfortunate because both young people exposed to adversity and their parents keenly want to know what they can do to mitigate their risk for depression or other adverse outcomes. Interestingly, epigenetic effects also illustrate how depression risk might be undone. A study with rats found that parenting behaviors can also stop a fire: When a female rat takes good care of her offspring, her pups are able to cope better with stress later in life compared to rat pups that were ignored and had high levels of stress. Remarkably, this improved coping was explained by lasting genetic changes in the well-cared-for pups (the bright side of epigenetics).

Fleshing out why risk becomes depression in some cases and why other children go on to live happy lives despite risk exposure is of paramount importance. Studying resilient children might uncover a specific set of behaviors (cognitions or actions) that help keep these youth well. We might even be able to teach these behaviors to other at-risk youth to prevent depression from taking hold.

8

DEPRESSION THROUGHOUT THE LIFE COURSE

Can children have depression?

Youth should be a time of frolic, play, and growth. The very idea of depressed children is tragic. In the 1970s and 1980s, there was debate among mental health authorities about whether children could experience clinical depression. That debate is over. Although childhood depression is not nearly as common as depression in adolescence and adulthood, unfortunately, it exists.

According to the National Health and Nutrition Examination Survey, approximately 2% of 8- to 11-year-olds are depressed in any given year. The Centers for Disease Control and Prevention estimates that between 1 in 200 and 1 in 50 U.S. children aged 3–6 years have major depression. Depression in toddlerhood is less common, although data for the youngest children remain scarce.

Beyond the fact that children can be depressed, we know much less about childhood depression than what we know about adolescent and adult depression. There aren't many surveys. Child populations are more difficult to enroll in research than adults. Assessing children (and adolescents) is also more challenging than assessing adults, so estimates of pediatric depression are more error-prone.

When we talk about moods in children, we have to remember that children are creatures of the moment: Parents and clinicians struggle to get a fix on child behavior as it flits about from hour to hour or even minute to minute. With the appearance of an ice cream cone, kids can veer from the depths of despair to flying high. Because children live in the now, they are less able to accurately report on their past mood or activities. Their vocabulary of mood concepts is smaller. Indeed, one reason people doubted that younger children could experience clinical depression was because symptoms such as guilt require greater conceptual sophistication or self-awareness than children typically have. Younger children have more trouble expressing what they are feeling in words than do older children or adults. Instead of saying they are sad, younger children may cling to a parent and refuse to be separated for fear of something bad happening; in other instances they may complain of vague physical ailments or refuse to attend school or leave the home.

Nevertheless, the official symptoms of childhood depression are essentially the same as those for older populations, with the addition of irritability, considered to be a symptom of depression in children. The duration of child depression is also similar to that of older populations. Although we are still learning about the causes of childhood depression, it is reasonable to assume that many of the contributing factors are similar to those of adolescent and adult depression—with biological, environmental, social, and cognitive factors topping the list.

Giving a child a psychiatric diagnosis is a serious matter and, to do it properly, also a taxing one. Diagnosing a child requires more data than required for an adult diagnosis. A strong clinician will try to obtain multiple perspectives on a child's behavior—starting with the child's perspective but also including those of the parents and the school (e.g., a teacher). In some cases, information from friends or classmates may also be useful. The clinician will have to synthesize these perspectives even though they often are in disagreement, knowing that many children act differently when they are in different contexts. Indeed, concerns about depression in a child are most heightened when there are consistent signs of depression across contexts (home, school, and friends) and over time (week to week). All children get sad. What warrants further evaluation by a pediatrician or mental health professional is when that sadness becomes persistent and when it interferes with a child's normal social activities, interests, schoolwork, or family life.

For many children, depression will just be a passing cloud. For others, depression will have enduring consequences. The serious outcomes associated with childhood depression are sobering. Depression can impair how a child interacts with peers, set back emotional growth, and hinder school performance. In addition, depression is a major contributing factor to suicide, the number three cause of death for preteens aged 11 and 12 years. For parents who want the best for their children and want to protect them from harm, this is scary stuff. Fear of the worst or of what others might think may explain why some parents deny the reality of their child's depression or delay seeking help for it.

Parents need to be reassured on two points. It is okay to seek help for their child's depression. And many depressed children can benefit from treatment. One caveat is that treatments for childhood depression are less extensively researched than adult treatments. For example, antidepressant medications were originally developed for adults, and what data we have indicate that these drugs may not be as effective for children. Likewise, established psychologically based therapies such as cognitive–behavioral therapy were also originally developed for adults. Although treatments for child depression are not always as powerful as we would like, and there is no consensus on the best way to modify adult treatments for children, it is also clear that treatments for child depression can be successful. The best first step for parents is to speak with a qualified child psychiatrist or child psychologist about what might work for their child.

Why does depression spike during adolescence?

Adolescence is a risky developmental period for depression. Surveys across several different countries find that 15–25% of adolescents have already had an episode of clinical depression. Adolescents, over their short lives, have experienced as much depression as adults. Why?

Adolescence is a life period when many things change simultaneously. The brain is developing rapidly. It is in a kind of neural no-man's-land, lacking the adult brain's self-control and still retaining the child brain's emotionality. Adolescents are diving headfirst into an intensely social world. Peers are becoming more influential; many teens are launching into intimate relationships often at the same time that they are starting to pull away from parents. Identity is uncertain and in flux. Adolescents may assert themselves by taking "adult risks," with forays into dangerous driving and drugs or alcohol.

The average adolescent is a little fragile, moody, and unsure. At this delicate developmental moment, it is easy for environmental threats to set depression in motion. Some teens develop depression after being bullied or ostracized. Others become depressed after a romantic rejection. For still others, it is a significant family stress such as a parental divorce that sets depression into motion. School difficulties can also be a trigger, especially as academic pressures mount for young people who perceive declining economic opportunities. Some unlucky youth confront several of these stressors simultaneously. And for adolescents with pre-existing vulnerability to depression, such as a genetic risk, or exposure to childhood adversity, there is great peril.

Girls are more likely to be swept up in these currents than are boys. In many ways, the story of adolescent depression is the rise of female depression. The major sex difference in depression originates in adolescence. In childhood, boys and girls report depression at approximately the same rates. By early to mid-adolescence, girls begin to evidence more depression than boys, and this difference increases throughout adolescence until it reaches the 2:1 ratio that typifies the rest of the life span.

Depression piggybacks on several dynamics that are worse for girls. The adolescent desire to be physically attractive, for one, is more intense for girls. In some studies, nearly 80% of adolescent girls (compared with 40% of adolescent boys) express dissatisfaction with their physical appearance. Physical appearance issues are especially difficult for early maturing girls who may face extra pressure to make themselves appealing to boys. Body image problems and weight concerns propel girls toward depression; they also propel girls toward eating disorders such as anorexia nervosa or bulimia—conditions that burgeon at this time of life.

Likewise, most teens recoil when they are excluded from fun or ridiculed for how they dress or how they look. This process, too, is tougher for girls: Considerable data indicate that adolescent girls are more sensitive to receipt of negative social feedback compared to boys. The harms of negative social feedback are also magnified for adolescent girls because of their higher engagement on social media. Constant use of Facebook, Instagram, or TikTok makes it easier to compare oneself to others or to conclude that one is not pretty enough, rich enough, or popular enough. Constant negative social comparisons enable negative thinking to take root. Consistent with this idea, large studies such as the Monitoring the Future survey find that teens who engage in the most screen activities such as social media and texting are the most unhappy. Conversely, teens who spend more time on nonscreen activities such as sports or homework tend to have lower levels of depression.

For the foreseeable future, the surge of adolescent depression will be a major public health concern worldwide. Adolescent depression not only harms the social, educational, and psychological development of youth but also is more likely than not to recur in adulthood. Fortunately, adolescent depression is as treatable (or even more so) than childhood depression. Parents should not hesitate to have their teen evaluated by a mental health professional. National data suggest that less than half of adolescents with depression receive any kind of mental health treatment.

As important as it is to get more individual youth into treatment, containing the epidemic of adolescent depression will require broader thinking. Key challenges include

- helping teens and adults better identify the signs of depression and better their abilities to engage in mental health dialogue;
- identifying strategies to prevent first episodes of depression in youth, including better identification of youth who are at risk;
- developing universal programs that help teens take better care of their mental health, including material delivered in schools; and
- finding ways to harness smartphone technology so it contributes to mental health rather than detracting from it, including designing mental health apps that appeal to teens.

Why are women more likely than men to have depression?

The sex difference in adult depression is one of the "big facts" about depression. This difference is generally observed throughout the world, including in one study of 25 European countries. It is observed across the whole age span of adulthood, across ethnicities, and it transcends social classes. Explaining this robust difference is one of the most important tasks of research.

No single reason can fully explain why women experience more depression compared to men. Many different reasons contribute.

There are obvious biological differences between men and women. Surprisingly, these differences do not appear to be a major explanation for why women have more depression compared to men. For example, there is little evidence that differences in sex hormones explain why depression is elevated in women. Likewise, male brains and female brains may differ in subtle ways, but such differences do not appear to be candidates for explaining sex differences in adult depression. Scientists are not even certain if there is a good biological explanation for the depression that affects some women at specific moments, such as phases of the menstrual cycle or after childbirth (postpartum depression).

The cultural and psychosocial differences between men and women appear to be better explanations. For example, men and women differ in how they communicate about emotion, with women having a more open communication style compared to men. Part of why women are more often diagnosed with depression could flow from their greater willingness and ability to report on depression. Stereotypically, men are less comfortable voicing difficult emotion. If males deny having depression, a psychological problem might manifest in alternative ways. For example, substance use problems are more common in men, and some hypothesize that a proportion of men struggling with a depressed mood drink alcohol or use drugs to cope instead of voicing their symptoms. Nevertheless, sex differences in how depression is reported are not the whole story. In some contexts, men are just as likely as women to report on mood problems. Notably, there is no sex difference in bipolar I disorder (the mood disorder that typically involves periods of mania and depression).

Another explanation is that women are exposed to a greater amount of stress and strain. Generally, women have lower power and lower status than do men. Objectively, women have lower incomes, as reflected in higher rates of poverty, compared to men. Women continue to face greater economic pressure and have greater strain in their roles. At work, women are more likely to be subject to harassment than are men. Women are more likely than men to face the mental and physical challenge of simultaneously performing paid work and caring for children (and increasingly caring for other relatives, such as aging parents).

Perhaps most ominously, women are more likely than men to be subjected to physical and sexual abuse, including rape. Women are much more likely than men to be battered in relationships, and women are at least twice as likely as men to be sexually assaulted. Sexual assault is known to be a strong antecedent of depression, particularly when it happens during childhood. By one estimate, up to 35% of the gender differences in adult depression could be attributed to the higher rate of childhood sexual assault experienced by girls.

Women face a variety of extra stressors; female psychology may make women particularly vulnerable to social stressors. Women are more interpersonally oriented than are men. This means that women are more likely than men to subordinate their psychological needs to others and even to be excessively dependent on others. Being interpersonally oriented makes it more likely for a woman to go into a tailspin after a relationship conflict or the end of a relationship. Epidemiologist Ronald Kessler has called this paradox the "cost of caring." Women have larger social networks compared to men. Although one would expect that it is beneficial to have a larger network of people who are mutually concerned for one another, for women, a larger network may not be so beneficial: across a larger network people are more likely to be impact by negative events, resulting in women being upset more frequently.

Exposure to excessive stress is probably not the entire story of sex differences, either. The ways women respond to stress may also be critical for explaining why stress readily becomes depression for women. We have already discussed rumination as a counterproductive response style. This ruminative tendency to turn inward and self-focus when sad is more common among women, and it is likely one way that depressive cognitions and mood may take hold after stress.

Throughout adulthood, women are more likely to have a history of depression than are men. It is possible that sex differences in depression are maintained over the life course simply because depression takes on its own momentum over time. For example, depression takes a toll on relationships, occupational functioning, and finances; these psychosocial problems in turn render a person more susceptible to having future depression. It is also possible that episodes of depression initiate biological changes that make depression more likely to recur in the future. The momentum of depression may explain part of why women experience more depression at any given point of the adult life span compared to men.

Although we know much about the sex difference in depression, critical questions remain:

- If socioeconomic inequalities explain part of why women are more vulnerable to depression, would achieving greater gender equality in one or more areas narrow the depression gap?
- Could it be possible to reduce sex differences in depression by reducing exposure to sexual violence in childhood or by making psychological services more readily available to victims?
- Could it be possible to develop psychological countermeasures for preventing depression in women—for example, by discouraging rumination or teaching women to be less interpersonally dependent?

It is clearly worth dedicating more research and treatment resources to combat depression in women. At the same time, it would be a mistake to neglect male depression. Male depression can get swept under the rug because it is less common. Men who struggle often try to hide it. Depression is perceived as "unmanly." Yet, male depression affects millions and can be deadly. In fact, although women are more likely to attempt suicide, men are more likely to die by suicide because men use more lethal means.

What is depression like in older people?

Older people inevitably face serious losses—of vitality, health, seeing contemporaries die. One might then think that old age is also a period of inevitably rising depression as well. Surprisingly, that is not the case.

Community-dwelling older persons have less clinical depression compared to their younger counterparts. When depression does occur in older persons, it is often related to ill-health and functional disability. Older persons who are hospitalized or who live in institutions such as nursing homes have markedly elevated rates of depression relative to older persons living independently.

Why might community-dwelling older persons have less depression than stereotypes about old age suggest? One possibility is that over time, older persons learn to become better at regulating their moods. Some researchers, such as psychologist Laura Carstensen, believe that as time left in life grows shorter, older persons develop a cognitive orientation that leads them to focus on short-term positive emotional goals, such as building close relationships. This tendency to focus on meaningful emotional goals may be protective against depression. Another possibility is that observed rates reflect a generational effect—stemming from the unique life experiences of older persons living now. Could it be, for example, that formative experiences such as growing up after World War II or coming of age into a relatively booming economy formed a psychology that was relatively resistant to depression? This generational hypothesis is difficult to test. However, if it is correct, the lower rates of depression in the current group of older persons will prove to be an anomaly and not persist in the next generation that comes of old age.

Depression in older persons has many of the same causes as depression in younger persons, such as major life stress and negative cognitions. Social contributions, such as isolation, or the death of a spouse, sibling, or close friend often loom large in geriatric depression. Nevertheless, depression in old age has some unique properties.

One unique challenge is demarcating where age-related challenges end and the symptoms of depression begin. For example, fatigue is very common in older persons, yet fatigue has many explanations that are unrelated to depression. Likewise, older persons can experience cognitive problems, such as difficulties concentrating or making decisions, for a number of reasons apart from depression. It's understandable when older people or their loved ones simply aren't sure whether depression might be a problem.

Relatedly, several age-related health problems are difficult to disentangle from depression. For example, older persons often take medications for health problems, and these medications can potentially induce depression as a side effect. For this reason, in the elderly, any change in type or dose of medication should be evaluated as a possible cause of depression symptoms. Age-related health conditions can produce depression directly. For instance, dementia often brings depression with it, as a direct consequence of the brain's deterioration. This is particularly true of vascular dementia, also known as stroke, and of Alzheimer's disease.

Disentangling depression from other age-related problems so depression can be treated appropriately is worth the effort. For instance, it is not uncommon for severely depressed older persons to present with a picture of cognitive decline. Loved ones may witness forgetfulness, confusion, and illogical thinking, and they may fear that an inevitable process of cognitive decline has begun. However, when the depression is treated and begins to improve, the cognitive impairments are completely reversed!

Perhaps because of these complications, depression in older persons is more likely to be seen and treated in medical settings, such as a primary care provider's office. Often in these contexts, assessment of depression is cursory. Weak assessment can lead to overdiagnosis and needless prescription of antidepressants—such as when relatively normal signs of aging and minor complaints are too easily attributed to depression. A hasty assessment can also lead to underdiagnosis and undertreatment, such as when the symptoms of depression are incorrectly attributed to another health problem or when the clinician discounts the older person's symptoms (e.g., "She is just lonely"). When assessments are less than ideal, family members can play a constructive role by providing more information to the doctor about the patient's history or current situation or by helping secure a second opinion.

Because depressed older people are very often cared for in medical settings, biological treatments such as antidepressants are by far the most common. For severe depression or depression with psychosis, electroconvulsive therapy (ECT), sometimes maligned as "shock" treatment, is used fairly often among older populations. Although ECT is often effective in bringing more rapid relief of symptoms compared to antidepressants (and speed is a valid consideration in an elderly person), a caveat with this treatment is the possibility of short-term memory loss, a concerning and relatively common side effect.

Depressed older people are less prone to seek out mental health care services and may not know about other treatment options aside from medications. This is unfortunate. Contrary to the idea that it is not possible to "teach an old dog new tricks," our best evidence indicates that psychologically based treatments, such as cognitive–behavioral therapy and interpersonal therapy, can be effective for older persons. This is good reason—whether you are an older person struggling with depression or care about one who is—to make use of the full array of treatments available for depression.

9

DEPRESSION OVER TIME

If I have depression, will it come back?

Jen is a 50-year-old school teacher who got depressed during her summer vacation. Was it all the unstructured time? Was it that her good friends were away on holiday and she felt left behind? Was it her parents' health, which had taken a turn for the worse? Jen had struggled with the blues before, but it was never this bad. So, she decided it was time to finally meet her mood issues head on and call a therapist. Perhaps seeing Dr. Glick made a difference. Because now it's fall and she's back in the classroom and feeling much like her normal self. At her next appointment, Jen asks a potentially loaded question: "Do you think my depression will come back?" Dr. Glick pauses before answering.

Jen's therapist is well-versed in the scientific literature on depression. In the fields of epidemiology and public health, predictive statements about depression tend to be pessimistic. The following statement from the pages of the prestigious medical journal, *The Lancet*, is typical: "Without treatment, depression has the tendency to assume a chronic course, be recurrent, and over time to be associated with increasing disability."[1]

---

1 Moussavi, S., Chatterji, S., Verdes, E., Tandon, A., Patel, V., & Ustun, B. (2007). Depression, chronic diseases, and decrements in health: Results from the World Health Surveys. *Lancet, 370,* 851–858.

Some data offer reason for pessimism. For example, one influential study followed a group of 380 individuals who recovered from an index major depressive episode for up to 15 years; in this sample, virtually all—nearly 9 in 10 people—had a recurrence of depression. Other epidemiological and long-term follow-up studies reinforce the idea that people who have had severe depression or who have had multiple episodes of depression are very likely to have future recurrences. By some accounts, recurrence of depression is the norm; an average person with depression could expect between five and nine episodes.

What happens to the average person may be good to know, but that is not the question at hand. Jen wants to know what every person with depression wants to know, which is: Will *my* depression recur? Her therapist takes a moment to ponder. Dr. Glick knows that the database on the long-term prognosis of depression has major gaps. The largest gap concerns depression in the *general* population—it is rare for scientific studies to be based on samples that represent all people who have depression. Most of what we know about depression in the long term comes from groups of people who sought treatment for depression (clinical samples). All things being equal, a person in a clinical sample is more severely affected than the average depressed person. Clinical samples by definitions, represent depressions that were severe enough or long lasting enough that the person sought help. Other long-term studies examine hospitalized inpatients, who likely represent the most severe cases of all, and who might naturally be expected to struggle with the disorder well after release.

Dr. Glick knows that only a handful of studies have examined the long-term course of depression in general population samples, which mirror all people with the disorder. Importantly, this work suggests a far more hopeful prognosis. In three major studies using general population samples, 40–60% of people who had a first episode of depression never experienced a recurrence, even after many decades of follow-up.

Staring at Jen, Dr. Glick hesitates for a few more moments. An answer is challenging because a clear-eyed look at our knowledge base suggests that there not one but two pattens of depression prognosis. It is as if two different boats of depressed people set sail in opposite directions. One group of depressed boaters is relatively recurrence prone. This boat sails into the future, and choppy seas are expected, with depression episodes recurring repeatedly over the life course. The second group of boaters enjoys much calmer waters—a smooth ride with no future episodes. A major review concluded that these boats were equal in size: "Approximately half of the people who suffer a major depressive episode for the first time experience recurrences, while the other half does not."[2]

Which boat was Jen in? And if you've had depression, how can you assess your chances of recurrence? Is it as uncertain as flipping a coin? Not exactly. We know several patterns are associated with recurrence.

You're more likely to experience recurrence if you have

- depression that started in childhood;
- other people in your family who are affected by depression;
- a history of physical or sexual abuse;
- ongoing medical problems, such as cardiovascular disease or diabetes;
- other mental health problems, such as anxiety; and
- mood problems that coincide with seasonal changes (low mood in the winter).

In addition, if you have already had several recurrences, a further recurrence is much more likely, with a briefer well period between depression episodes. Scientists are still trying to

2 Monroe, S. M., Anderson, S. F., & Harkness, K. L. (2019). Life stress and major depression: The mysteries of recurrences. *Psychological review*, 126, 791.

understand why it is that recurrence seems to initiate processes that escalate depression risk. Some researchers, for instance, have postulated that recurrences of depression cause biologically based changes in the central nervous system that enhance future risk. It is important to improve our predictions of *who* will experience recurrence and *why*. Such improvement would allow us to develop tests that enable us to better predict and track a person's risk for recurrence. Ideally, such knowledge would be used to develop new ways to intervene to stave off a recurrence before it occurs.

For people who have experienced multiple episodes of depression, please do not lose hope. Importantly, it is possible to improve your long-term outcome via a "maintenance" treatment. Maintenance treatment is ongoing, often open-ended therapy that continues even after an episode of depression has resolved. Maintenance treatment is expressly designed to reduce risk for future recurrences. Two forms of maintenance treatment that are known to significantly reduce rates of depression recurrence are antidepressant medications and continuation treatment with psychologically based therapy, such as cognitive–behavioral therapy. There are indications that the best protection against recurrence is obtained by combining medication and psychologically based therapy.

If you have had only a single episode of depression, can you ever breathe a sigh of relief about your future risk? In some cases, yes. Based on what we know, you are less likely to have further depression episodes if

- your depression was brief and lasted less than 6 months;
- your depression occurred many years ago and you have been well since;
- your occupational and social functioning was good before depression started;
- the depression was due to an obvious stressor and the event is now completely resolved; and
- your medical and psychological health are otherwise good.

Dr. Glick breaks the silence,

> While there are no guarantees, Jen, you definitely have a lower risk for recurrence than average; fortunately, your episode was relatively brief and it responded well to treatment, and your depression wasn't complicated by other medical or psychological problems. People who have this sort of profile tend to do well. We will keep in touch of course, but I am optimistic.

Jen smiles. Time will tell.

What is chronic depression?

Most people who have depression will eventually recover. On average, depression episodes last approximately 6 months. However, this also means that a minority of people do not recover from depression, even over very long follow-up periods. Long-term follow-up studies find that 10–15% of initially depressed persons still have not recovered 10–15 years later.

The dogged persistence of depression is one of the major challenges for persons struggling with the condition and also for their loved ones. For 18 months, John had put his life on hold as his depression raged. He did not make any major decisions. He wanted to get married and start a family, but in his current state, he did not dare ask his girlfriend to be his wife. John's parents kept telling him it would get better. Therapists and psychiatrists likewise counseled patience. So much waiting. Yet depression did not relent.

The *Diagnostic and Statistical Manual of Mental Disorders* (DSM) considers depressions that last more than 2 years to be chronic, a designation called persistent depressive disorder. John's depression would have to continue for another 6 months to meet the formal criteria for chronic depression.

Chronic depressions are by no means rare—some estimates are that 30% of depressions in the community could be considered chronic.

Many of the same things that predict recurrent depression also predict chronic depression, such as

- childhood maltreatment;
- co-occurring mental health problems, including personality disorders, anxiety disorders, and substance use disorders; and
- elevated rates of depression among family members.

Chronic depression also connects to personality dispositions or patterns of behavior that emerge from inborn childhood temperaments. Temperaments are one source of continuity of human behavior. All things being equal, shy children are more likely to become shy adults, whereas outgoing children are more likely to become outgoing adults. In the case of depression, temperamental dispositions to experience more negative emotion and less positive emotion put a person at greater risk for chronic depression during the life course.

John, in some ways, fits a depression-prone temperamental profile. He remembers how he stood apart from other kids from an early age. He remembers how he laid awake at night, thinking about the end of the world. John remembers when his third grade teacher poked fun at him and called him a worrier. He remembers how he drove himself to achieve during his school years, and no matter how many trophies or straight A's he received, John could never be satisfied. John wonders (and worries) that his lifelong tendency to brood and expect the worst may now be feeding his depression.

Recurrence and chronicity are distinct aspects of depression. Some people have many recurrences of depression without any of the episodes becoming chronic. Others might have a chronic depression that does not recur. Even so, chronicity and recurrence are interrelated. Many of the factors that predict a depression being more chronic also predict depression recurrence (e.g., life stress). Scientists are continuing to investigate the interrelationships between chronicity and recurrence. For example, in many studies, depressed persons who have more chronic symptoms and do not completely recover from depression are much more likely to have recurrence, including relapse and occurrence of future depression episodes.

Is there such a thing as a depressive personality?

Personality refers to general patterns of thought, emotion, cognition, and motivation. When we talk about people as being honest, curious, agreeable, or friendly, this is the language of personality traits. Is there such a thing as a depressive personality? Not exactly. There is no single personality that gets depressed. Introverts can be depressed. And so can extraverts. Agreeable people can get depressed. And so can disagreeable people.

For a time, there was a diagnostic category called depressive personality disorder that was being studied for inclusion as an official diagnostic category. This referred to people who

- are typically gloomy or cheerless in their mood;
- conceive of themselves as inadequate;
- tend to be critical and self-blaming;
- tend to be negative and judgmental toward others;
- are pessimistic about the future; and
- are prone to guilt or remorse.

Despite some evidence of a group of people who possess these traits, and despite evidence that people with these traits are more prone to depression, this category was ultimately decommissioned from the DSM. There was just not enough evidence to retain it.

There is no single depressive personality type. However, the idea that depression is in some way related to personality is worth entertaining. There are both pros and cons to the concept of a depressive personality.

Regarding the pros, first it is true that some personality styles are more prone to develop episodes of depression than others. We saw that in links between temperamental dispositions and chronic depression. We saw that with the proposed diagnosis of depressive personality disorder, which captured a group of individuals who were more likely to struggle with depression episodes. The most powerful demonstrations of the power of personality come from several studies that linked personality traits in childhood to the development of depressive disorders in adults. In one study, children who were rated as socially reticent, inhibited, and easily upset at the age of 3 years demonstrated elevated rates of depressive disorders at age 21 years. In another investigation, physicians' ratings of behavioral apathy at ages 6, 7, and 11 years predicted both adolescent mood disorder and chronic depression in middle adulthood.

Regarding the cons, first the strength of this evidence is modest and it is dangerous to exaggerate it. Personality—even as it might indicate who is more likely to develop depression— isn't destiny. For example, many children who are reticent, inhibited, or easily upset never develop depression.

One reason why personality might not predict depression is that our personality traits are not etched in stone. Personality can change over the life course. It is possible for a reticent child to turn into an outgoing adult, and many do. Others might become more shy with age. Life experiences are among the factors that can alter personality, and depression may be one of these life experiences. Several studies of personality have found that people who experienced depression rate their personality characteristics differently after the episode of depression than they did before the episode. Another caveat is that the depressed state can also bias how people evaluate their personality. John, 18 months into his depression, has difficulty thinking of the many periods in his life when he was not depressed. Because his depression has lasted so long, he comes to believe "I've always been this way," viewing himself as generally pessimistic, guilt prone, and cheerless. His girlfriend fights this theory. She reminds him of what he was really like 2 years ago; she brings out tokens of the former John—the photo albums from their trips together and his effervescent courtship letters. John doesn't recognize that fellow.

A final con of depressive personality is that the concept of depressive personality may itself be harmful. For example, the concept of depressive personality may lead people to be fatalistic in the face of depression. When John believes he has a depressive personality, this belief undermines his efforts to explore behaviors that could lift him out of his episode. He insists, "There's nothing I can do. It's just how I am." The idea of depressive personality may also adversely impact how others interact with a depressed person. For instance, when people view depression as coming from a person's essential nature, they may be inclined to "blame" the depressed person for their episode. This kind of finger pointing benefits no one. In this respect, perhaps it's a good thing that the data on depressive personality are not very strong.

10

WHY IS THERE AN EPIDEMIC OF DEPRESSION?

A mood science approach to the depression epidemic

Chapter 4 presented evidence that rates of depression have increased in the past generation, particularly among younger people. How can we explain this? Surprisingly, the task is challenging. Part of the challenge is that there are many possible candidate factors in the modern environment—such as political changes, economic changes, and cultural changes—all operating simultaneously. Life is not a controlled experiment. It can be difficult to determine which factors are relevant and which ones are not.

Our mood science approach may be particularly helpful for zeroing in on some of the key factors that may be responsible for contemporary spikes in depression. In this approach, we consider the design of the mood system, the forces that act on mood, and the ways our species has altered those forces, often dramatically. No one should pretend this is a definitive proof, or even an exhaustive explanation. Nevertheless, I believe there was and is a persuasive case to make, and readers who want more detail on these issues are referred to my book, *The Depths: The Evolutionary Origins of the Depression Epidemic* (Basic Books, 2014).

It is important to bear in mind that mood is a primitive adaptation built into our very makeup and that moods, both low and high, often serve us well, even now. The question is whether our mood system is perfectly suited for modernity. In just a few hundred generations, humans colonized the planet, built cities, and invented technologies beyond the wildest dreams of those who lived in earlier times. The dizzying speed of change in our physical and cultural environment has only accelerated in the past generation, outmatching the pace of evolution of our nervous systems to keep up. The conditions of modern life have sent low mood into overdrive. A perfectly good adaptation in a less revved-up and stimulating world may now be out of step with the demands of modern life.

In short, our modern environment is terrible for mood. What this means in practice is that a greater proportion of people are in a low mood for a longer period of time. How an epidemic of low mood translates into an epidemic of depression is straightforward. With increasingly more people struggling with periods of low mood, millions teeter near the brink of more serious depression. With a small push, that low mood descends more deeply a more disabling and more distressing clinical depression. For some, it's adversity—such as trouble at work—that does the pushing. Others are pushed over by a biological vulnerability to depression. For still others, it's negative thinking patterns that join with environmental forces to seed the ground for clinical depression.

How modern routines disturb mood

Modern routines wreak havoc on mood. A good example involves altered patterns of light exposure. Light matters because our mood system evolved in the context of a rotating earth, with its recurrent 24-hour cycle of light and dark phases. Our species is diurnal, and historically the best chance of finding sustenance and other rewards was in the light phase, in sunshine, during the day (good luck identifying edible berries or tracking a buffalo by moonlight!). Naturally, we are configured to be more alert during the day than at night.

Consistent with links between light and mood, many people experience low mood when seasonal change brings shorter daylight hours. In fact, especially sensitive persons might experience *seasonal affective disorder*, a subtype of mood disorder, which is usually at its worst during winter.

Modern technology has dramatically transformed our species' light exposure. With the advent of electricity, our species has increasingly relied on indoor light. And with urbanization, increasingly fewer people engage in occupations such as farming that take place in the outdoors. Artificial light is a poor substitute for the Sun: It is much fainter and provides fewer mood benefits. Studies with small devices that measure human light exposure document that modern citizens don't get enough. of it: Even people who live in sunny locations such as San Diego, California, receive less than 1 hour of sunlight a day. Low levels of daily light exposure among those studied relate directly to the experience of low mood. In this sense, human ingenuity has inadvertently led our species into darkness.

Another way that modern lighting conditions disturb mood is through disrupted sleep routines, critical as we appreciate just how foundational a good night's sleep is to mood. A problem with our love of artificial light is that the exposure occurs at the wrong time. Rather than sunlight during the day (as preferred by our mood system), we get ersatz light at night. Artificial light exposure bouncing off TVs, iPads, or cell phone screens wreaks havoc with our internal body clocks, which set our 24-hour mood rhythms of sleep and waking. Artificial light essentially tricks the body into staying awake, delaying the onset of sleep. Not only is this light bad for our body clock but also it is connected to psychologically stimulating activities that delay sleep. Whether it is texting, binging on shows, or videogaming, activities on light-emitting devices keep people awake deep into the night. Writ large, excess light and light-related activities at night have spawned an epidemic of poor sleep.

Sleep survey data suggest a population less well rested than it once was; by some estimates, people get 90 minutes of sleep less now than they did in 1900. Alarmingly, more than 40% of Americans between the ages of 13 and 64 years say they rarely or never get a good night's sleep on weeknights, and a third of young adults probably have long periods of at least partial sleep deprivation on an ongoing basis. You may know from personal experience that when you sleep poorly, your mood is low. Consistent with this common experience, sleep scientists have documented the tight connections between impairments in the quality and quantity of sleep and the tendency to experience depressed mood during waking hours.

Does social media play a role?

Thus far, I have gently pointed a finger at modern technologies for population-level changes in mood. Are we too quick to blame technology? There's a long tradition dating back to Luddites smashing factory machines where technology is scapegoated for every social ill. In recent years, among the most vilified technologies are popular social media platforms such as Facebook or Instagram. These platforms have been connected to a host of social maladies, including the devolution of public discourse, bullying, the rise of eating disorders, and even mass violence. So perhaps it's no surprise: Social media use has also been connected to the contemporary depression epidemic. Is there any foundation for this idea?

It is plausible that increased use of social media might play a role in depression. As discussed previously, the mood system closely tracks the social world, including the health of our major relationships and how others view us. The rise of social media certainly has implications for mood because in short order, these platforms have transformed how and where people interact with one another to the point where virtual interactions and virtual perceptions can be as or more important than those of real life. For example, one recent study estimated that just since 2012, the amount of time teenagers spend on social networking sites has risen 62.5%. The trend toward moving social life online has only accelerated with the COVID-19 pandemic.

The most recent scholarly reviews suggest that social media use can be harmful to mood: When all the research studies are combined in a meta-analysis, the results indicate that those who are spending more time on social network sites and are more often checking social media accounts are reporting higher levels of depression. Interestingly, depression is also connected to a greater tendency to compare oneself to others, which one might say is the essential point of social networking sites.

These results are not a smoking gun that proves that using Facebook makes you more depressed. If fact, these findings raise as many questions as they answer about the precise nature of the relationship between social media platforms and depression. Is there anything in social media platforms that is inherently dangerous to mood? Or are the platforms neutral for mood but misused in ways that promote depression? Or might it simply be that people who are struggling with their mood are particularly drawn to use these platforms? One of the most compelling ideas is that social media outlets such as Facebook and Instagram have turbocharged a new psychological race to keep up with the Joneses. In this view, people use these channels to relentlessly document their "highlight reels." Social media posts feature the bliss from vacations, newly acquired possessions, and parties with friends, with the more mundane parts of life largely edited out. Social media may harm mood when people inevitably compare their own lives unfavorably to the virtual Joneses—who are perceived as richer, more attractive, or more popular. This process, called upward social comparison—the tendency to reference other people's highlight reels—may help explain why heavy social media use is associated with low mood and depression. Social media use may put continuing pressure on mood when people heavily use social media, feel worse, yet feel compelled to continue to consume social media even more, further worsening mood.

It is also possible that constant social media use is changing culture in ways that facilitate low mood. Constant exposure to other people's highlight reels on social media might harm mood because it alters our conventions about what moods are normal to experience. The formal concept here is called meta-emotion, which involves peoples' beliefs about emotion, including beliefs about what is normal or desirable to feel. To the extent that reality is socially constructed, observing other people's bliss on social media may contribute to a shared illusion that other people are happier than they actually are. Believing that one is less happy than others is another unfortunate aspect of the psychological arms race to keep up with the Joneses.

Finally, the flip side of what is shared on social media is what is not shared there. What is not shared (or is not sharable) also has implications for depression. Living up to a carefully curated image of a perfect life may bring with it greater pressure to conceal depression, both on social media and in real life, and to push away support that might come from admitting vulnerability. If social interaction is increasingly mediated by social media and social media has limited space for discussing low mood and depression, it is easy to imagine that those with low mood may end up feeling more isolated and alone, opening up another path for depression to gestate.

The perils of a happiness-obsessed culture

Social media may also be symbolic of a larger cultural shift—a cultural obsession with happiness, an obsession that, ironically, may be another breeding ground for the depression epidemic. Throughout human history, there has never been available so much advice—spiritual, medical, psychological, and folk-inspired—about how to be happier than there is now. In the past 15 years, an ever-growing stream of psychological and popular science books examines happiness and how people can increase it. Ideally, these resources should serve as bulwarks against depression. Perversely, the opposite may be the case. Predominant cultural imperatives about what we should feel, although surely well-intentioned, may be worsening the depression epidemic.

Survey data show Westerners place a particularly high value on experiencing intense positive mood states. Positive states such as joy and affection have been rated as more desirable and appropriate in Australia and the United States than in Taiwan and China. What could ever be wrong with pursuing happiness to the fullest extent possible? A natural intuition is that the more you value your happiness, the happier you will be. Contemporary psychological research suggests that this intuition is mistaken: Fixating on happiness as a goal can backfire. The rise of unrealistic mood standards may be why so many people are chronically asking, "Why am I not happier?" and setting out to grasp an unattainable mood. Increasingly, there's a yawning gap between what we want to feel and what we actually feel—a chronic dissatisfaction that breeds depression.

The most compelling evidence for this happiness gap comes from a series of studies by Iris Mauss and colleagues at the University of California. These investigators have found that people who value happiness the most are actually the most depressed and have the greatest difficulty achieving well-being. In this way, the goal of becoming happier appears unlike other goals, such as learning to play the piano—where if you put your mind to it, sit at a piano, and "practice," you will get closer to the goal. Intensely wanting to become happier may instead be more like running on a treadmill that speeds up the faster you try to run.

Of course, no one wants to wallow in depression, yet it may be the case that our well-being would be higher if our culture set its sights for mood lower. There is evidence that when a person sets unrealistic goals for mood states, it is more difficult to accept or tolerate negative emotional experiences such as anxiety or sadness. Oddly, it's being able to accept negative feelings—rather than always striving to make them disappear—that seems to be associated with feeling better, not worse, over the long term. One theory is that when people accept negative feelings, those experiences draw less attention and less negative evaluation than they would otherwise. Some types of psychotherapy, such as acceptance and commitment therapy, have as an explicit aim to help people increase their ability to accept negative feelings when they arise. Consistent with this goal, those who report a more robust ability to "accept" unpleasant feelings are less likely to experience depressive symptoms in the future.

Young persons: The future of the depression epidemic?

Ominously, young people are at the epicenter of all the previously discussed trends—whether it is the use of electronics at night, poor sleep routines, heavy use of social media, upward social comparison, or adoption of unrealistic expectations for happiness. This confluence of forces among youngsters may help explain why this demographic faces so much depression. This concentration of depression among younger cohorts is one of the most disturbing omens of the depression epidemic. Depression is especially disruptive when it strikes people young, and early onset is, all things being equal, a predictor of depression recurrence.

Of course, what has happened already does not completely foretell what will happen in the future. There is no guarantee that observed trends in the depression epidemic will continue. Let's not declare any particular generation to be lost. This "perfect storm" for mood may subside, and rates of depression may plateau and even decline. In the future, technology may prove to be the friend of mood rather than its foe. Someday, scientists may be able to use information from the genome to deliver personalized mood treatments. Artificial intelligence may advance to the point that a first-rate mood coach will be available for everyone with a smartphone. Perhaps wide swaths of the population will tire and turn away from social media and the psychological arms race that run rampant on its networks.

Even if our world does not become friendlier toward mood, and even if depression continues as a pre-eminent mental health problem, as discussed later, all is not lost. There will still be actions the individual can take to be a better steward of mood for oneself or for a loved one.

PART III

REMEDIES FOR DEPRESSION

11

WHAT ARE MY TREATMENT OPTIONS?

What are the best treatments for depression?

Given how debilitating depression can be, you might think most who suffer from it seek professional help. That's far from the case, however. One nationwide study of more than 15,000 U.S. adults revealingly titled "Depression Care in the United States: Too Little for Too Few" found that only approximately half of people who struggled with depression in the past year received any form of treatment. Most troubling, only one out of five depressed persons received a treatment that satisfied recommended professional guidelines. This means that when depression is treated, it is often undertreated or is treated with unproven therapies.

There are undoubtedly many reasons for this bleak scorecard. For some people, entering treatment for depression, as for any mental health problem, is scary, like venturing inside a mysterious black box. Others may resist seeking professional help because they believe it marks a personal failure to solve depression on one's own. The cost of treatment—both real and perceived—can also be an obstacle. Finally, often people just lack the knowledge that's necessary to proceed with treatment: They don't know which treatments are effective or how to access such treatments. Mindful of the obstacles, this chapter presents a brief and sober overview of depression treatments, focusing on those that are most effective.

To state the conclusion at the outset, there's both good news and bad news about treatment for depression. The good news: Depression is indeed treatable. In fact, multiple depression treatments (we focus on three major treatments) have been shown in extensive and exhaustive research to reliably alleviate its symptoms. The bad news: Even the best depression treatments cannot be regarded as cures. On average, depression treatment yields only partial relief of symptoms. As frequently stated in car commercials, "Your mileage may vary." In the case of depression treatment, that mileage can vary from total relief to minimal benefit and even deterioration, in some cases. There is no quick fix. Getting well from depression requires persistence.

This chapter focuses on the three formal interventions that have the most established track records. We'll call them the big three.

Cognitive–behavioral therapy

Cognitive–behavioral therapy (CBT) is a form of psychotherapy for depression. More than 40 years of research document CBT's efficacy, with half or more of depressed patients who engage in this therapy experiencing significant symptom reductions (meaning symptoms are reduced by half or more). CBT is founded on the proposition that depression arises fundamentally from faulty thoughts and thinking patterns. A first goal of CBT is to help a person simply become more aware of their negative thinking patterns and habits. Once aware, the treatment program then provides a series of exercises that encourage the person to change these thinking patterns.

CBT is structured. This structure is reflected in (1) the specific training that CBT practitioners receive; (2) practitioners' use of a manual to guide sessions; and (3) the time-limited nature of treatment, with specific goals to be achieved in 8–16 sessions.

What do you do in CBT? CBT typically involves both activities in session and homework, which will allow you to continue your treatment outside of appointments. In CBT, you will

- learn to track your moods and thoughts in specific situations;
- be given exercises to challenge your typical thoughts;
- gain new tools for coping with your thoughts; and
- gain a better understanding of your "triggers."

CBT does not resemble the cartoons you may have seen of psychotherapy—the image of a person lying on a couch, musing about dreams or early childhood to a distant therapist who renders sage interpretations. Instead, CBT is practical (let's fix your cognitions), collaborative (the therapist freely shares details about the process), hands-on (do these homework exercises), and results-oriented (we expect to see progress in a matter of weeks). For many people, these aspects of CBT are refreshing.

Interpersonal psychotherapy

Since the 1970s, interpersonal psychotherapy (IPT) has been extensively and favorably evaluated as a treatment for depression. Its proven efficacy is similar to that of CBT. Despite IPT's excellent track record, many people don't know about it. IPT is an intervention that homes in on how people (including depressed people) function in their social relationships. IPT's premise is that the symptoms of depression typically stem from problems or difficulties in relating to others. IPT naturally begins with an assessment of the depressed person's social world, and what is discovered in that assessment informs what themes the therapist pursues in the ensuing treatment. For example, for one client, grief after a death might be the most salient theme. For another client, struggles with a changing social role (e.g., a young person leaving home for college) are critical. For still another, the central problem may be that important social relationships are filled with conflict (e.g., marital difficulty).

What do you do in IPT?

- Assess the health of your relationships and relationship patterns
- Recognize the connections between your relationships and the way you are feeling
- Work with the therapist on identifying and modifying one main relationship theme

Like CBT, IPT is time-limited and structured, typically unfolding over 12–16 weekly sessions. Also, like the CBT therapist, the IPT therapist is more interested in the present (your relationships now) than in what might have happened in the more distant past. Generally, going through IPT should be a pleasant experience. A well-trained therapist will display empathy and help the client feel understood while enabling work on social relationships. Common activities in IPT include boosting the client's ability to assert their needs and wishes in interpersonal encounters, helping the client understand that anger is a normal emotion and helping expressions of anger to be channeled in more constructive ways, encouraging the client to take appropriate social risks, and improving how the client grapples with social isolation and/or unfulfilling social relationships.

Medication treatments for depression

Antidepressants refer to a large group of medications that are prescribed to help reduce or control symptoms of depression. Although some of the drugs are new, many have been used for more than 50 years. Antidepressants often must be taken 2–4 weeks before they produce a therapeutic effect, and it may take up to 12 weeks to reach full effect. With the help of the prescriber, a patient may need to try various dosages or kinds of medication to find what works best for them. Even if antidepressants are less than a cure-all, these drugs have an extensive track record, and there is robust evidence that many people benefit from taking them.

What you can expect in antidepressant treatment?

- You will have your physical health evaluated.
- Your depression symptoms will be carefully evaluated.
- You will begin medication at a starting dose and adjust the dose as a function of side effects and whether a therapeutic response is observed.
- Your provider will periodically monitor your symptoms and adjust dosage or change medication based on whether your symptoms improve.

Sometimes, medication treatment is combined with some form of psychotherapy, which can be provided by the person prescribing or by another mental health professional.

In the United States, the U.S. Food and Drug Administration (FDA) has approved more than two dozen antidepressants, with similar numbers available in other countries. The multitude of available options poses the question of which to try first. Somewhat frustratingly, selecting an antidepressant remains largely a trial-and-error process. In choosing an antidepressant, the treating professional will consider what other antidepressants you have taken previously, potential side effects, other health conditions you may have, potential interactions with other medications you may be taking, as well as cost. As treatment progresses, the number of potential medication permutations becomes vast, as the prescriber may consider not only a sequence of single drugs but also combinations of drugs (known as augmentation strategies). One important strand of psychiatry research intends to more efficiently match patient characteristics to the drug or drugs that will work best. The results of research on matching have not been decisive, however. This leaves practitioners to rely largely on their own clinical experience in making these decisions.

The duration of medication treatment varies widely. Clinical studies most commonly evaluate medications for efficacy over the short term (e.g., 12 weeks). For people who are treated successfully, there is often a recommendation to continue taking the medications, known as maintenance treatment. Supporting maintenance, some longer term studies that follow patients for 1 year or longer find that continuation with antidepressants offers some protection against relapse relative to patients who do not continue a course of antidepressant treatment. For people who have had multiple depression episodes, many health professionals will recommend prolonged—and even lifetime—maintenance of antidepressant treatment as a means to keep symptoms from returning. Taking a drug for a lifetime is obviously a major decision—and so is stopping a drug that has been taken for a long time. Indeed, some popular press reports, and some research, indicate that there can be ill effects when these antidepressant medications are ceased abruptly—including an increased risk of depressive symptoms returning.

The original theories of antidepressants posited that these drugs reduce depression by altering neurotransmitter activity, the correction of a so-called chemical imbalance. These original theories have not held up well, and scientists are formulating more complex models of why the drugs work. What has not changed is the bottom line: These drugs are often helpful in combatting the symptoms of depression, which is often all the patient really wants to know.

Other important treatment options

People are less aware of medical treatment options for depression besides antidepressants. One important medical treatment is electroconvulsive therapy (ECT). ECT has a poor public image, denigrated as "shock treatment" and even depicted as a form of torture in popular films such as *One Flew Over the Cuckoo's Nest*. In fairness, electrocution is a frightening notion, and ECT was sometimes used indiscriminately in the past. Still, the bad reputation of ECT is unwarranted because the modern research base supports it as a surprisingly safe (the major dangers are the risks associated with anesthesia), well-studied, and well-controlled procedure, particularly for treating severe or treatment-resistant depression. ECT is often administered as a series of 6–12 treatments in which seizures are intentionally and briefly induced. ECT can be administered on an inpatient or outpatient basis. The disadvantages of ECT include that it is intensive and costly to deliver and that it can cause cognitive side effects (e.g., particularly a loss of memory for events around the time of the treatments). One of ECT's signal advantages is that it can work more rapidly than antidepressant medications; this speed of action is obviously appealing when a patient and/or their loved ones are desperate for help.

There are other promising, but not as well-validated, treatments worth mentioning in the discussion of more rapid-acting medical treatments. The first is transcranial magnetic stimulation (TMS). TMS is a noninvasive treatment that uses magnetic fields to stimulate nerve cells in the brain to improve symptoms of depression. The second is ketamine, a drug that is administered by intravenous infusion or nasal spray. Currently, much buzz and fanfare surround ketamine because the nasal spray form of the drug (esketamine) has been approved by the FDA for treatment-resistant depression. Efficacy data are not as well established for TMS or for ketamine as they are for the other treatments mentioned in this chapter. TMS and ketamine both represent options that might be considered when other measures have been exhausted. Issues of cost and access will need to be overcome before they become widely used depression treatments.

Finally, there are circumstances in which depression benefits from treatment in a hospital setting. Generally, hospitalization should be considered when depression is very severe, when the person is considered at a high risk of harming themselves or others, and/or when multiple other treatments have not worked. Hospitals can provide a good context for treating depression because they are safe places that allow both for more intensive treatment and for more intensive monitoring of treatment. The duration of a hospital stay for depression varies greatly (from days to weeks to even months), but stays are generally getting shorter as cost pressure mounts on health care actors. The ease of obtaining hospital treatment also varies widely, depending on the availability of health care, how health care is delivered and administered, and the laws regarding commitment.

How effective are different depression treatments?

The landscape of treatment for depression presents an odd state of affairs. An impressive array of established treatments have been shown incontrovertibly to reduce the symptoms of depression. Yet victory over depression also seems far out of reach. Nothing is close to being a cure that wipes out depression in the way that vitamin C wipes out scurvy. Rather, available depression treatments are *tools* to help people manage their depression symptoms and reduce these symptoms over time. Perhaps most frustrating of all is that our extensive knowledge about treatment does not generally tell us ahead of time *which treatment will be best for any given individual*, which is exactly what depressed people and their families most want to know.

These irksome gaps in our knowledge are in some ways understandable. Treatment research studies are incredibly resource-intensive undertakings. They require major investments of time, money, and personnel to perform. A good treatment study even of a single modality is already an achievement. Rare are large-scale studies that directly compare different treatment modalities with one another—studies that could demonstrate which treatment might be best overall or best for particular subgroups of patients. Unfortunately, the rare large-scale investigations that exist, such as the National Institute of Mental Health's Collaborative Research Program, did not arrive at conclusive findings. On the contrary, the scientists involved ended up arguing about aspects of the results for decades. Thus, the bottom line here is somewhat bland: Multiple treatments can help a person with depression, but we don't know necessarily which is best.

When viewed from our mood science perspective, the bland bottom line makes sense. A bedrock principle of the mood science perspective is that the mood system is open to multiple inputs. Just as we have highlighted the different roads that lead to depression, with treatment, what we see is the other side of the coin, with several different roads that lead out of depression. Among the validated roads are systematically changing your cognitions (CBT), your social interactions (IPT), and the chemicals inside your brain (antidepressants). Knowing that these roads exist, and that we may discover even more existing routes, is reassuring. This is a good fact to hold onto at moments when depression feels overwhelming or permanent.

How should I decide which treatment to try?

There is no single consideration that should dictate which treatment to try. After learning about the possibilities, it is fine to try the form of treatment that you most feel comfortable with. In the real world, cost and availability of treatment are also important factors. Before making a decision to proceed after an initial consultation with a treating professional, first consider whether you like the person and understand their treatment plan. In fact, treatment research indicates that liking and believing in a treatment and a treating professional are key factors that can facilitate the treatment's success.

Learning more about a therapist and addressing potential concerns about treatment can help you be more confident in moving forward. The following are questions you can ask at an initial visit:

- How long have you been practicing?
- What licenses and certifications do you have and which professional organizations do you belong to?
- How much do you charge? What are your sliding-scale options?
- How many clients have you had with similar circumstances to my own? When was the last time you worked with someone similar to me?
- Describe your ideal patient.
- Tell me a little about what I can expect in treatment.

Do your best to resist depression's pull toward fatalism and passivity as you approach treatment. You'll be best off if you take an active role in your own care. After all, it's your mood. People often think that managing moods is an either–or proposition with a stark choice between consulting a professional or going it alone. In the long term, you might consider the benefits of adopting a both–and approach—that is, taking what is useful from a trained professional while doing what you can do to manage your mood on top of that (see Chapter 12).

Depressed people often have anxiety about changing treatment. This anxiety is natural. As part of the more active approach, you should be patient with a treatment while at the same time being prepared to move on to another when you need to do so. For example, if you have tried a treatment for 2 or more months and you're not getting any better, this should be discussed plainly with your treating professional. A decision to change therapists or treatments should ideally be a joint one, but ultimately you are the one to make the final call.

How can I find a competent treating professional?

Finding a good professional who is experienced in treating depression is no small feat. The following are general recommendations about how to search:

- Word of mouth is a sound way to identify a good treatment professional. Your friends and family may have ideas, or your primary care doctor may be able to provide an initial referral.
- Contact the psychiatry department at a local medical school or a university psychology department and ask staff if they can recommend clinicians who are experienced at treating depression.
- Contact a local hospital for information about mental health clinics or recommendations of staff psychiatrists.
- National mental health organizations can also help with referral lists of licensed credentialed providers.
- If you know specifically that you want to try IPT or CBT for depression, a Web-based search using these terms may be able identify local providers who are trained in these modalities.
- When cost/insurance coverage is an issue, check out local senior centers, religious organizations, and community mental health clinics. Such places often offer therapy on a sliding scale for payment or may be able to refer you to treating professionals who do so.

Final quick pep talk: Top five reasons to consider treatment

People routinely consult professionals for help with a plumbing problem, a termite infestation, or for planning a fun wedding. From this standpoint, it is strange that anyone would be hesitant to consult a professional for help with the most profound and important of issues—one's mental health. In case you're still on the fence or need a pep talk, I offer my top five reasons to consider treatment for depression:

1. Depression can be very challenging to manage on your own. Use all the tools at your disposal.
2. Going into treatment is a proactive step, not an admission of defeat.
3. The inconvenience and cost of treatment are small relative to the possible benefits of controlling your depression.
4. You are not alone. Millions of people before you have tried CBT, IPT, and antidepressants, and most have benefited from these treatments.
5. You are worth it.

There are two meta messages in this chapter. First, treatment is not a one-time thing but is an extended process. Second, you will play a leading role in the process of gaining better control of your mood. You have already started the process. Buying this book and reading it to this point are steps in becoming more educated about mood and mood disorders. The next chapter brings home more fully what you can do to change mood.

12

WHAT CAN THE DEPRESSED PERSON DO FOR THEMSELF?

Start from where you are

You have arrived at this point in the book. You may be struggling with depression. You may have already tried several treatments. You may feel like nothing is working, or will ever work. What now?

You can do something for yourself. It is possible.

Saying that the individual can do things to influence depression does not mean that perfect control of depression is possible, that depressed people should be blamed when depression persists, or that changing mood is easy. Every human has at least some limited zone of control over mood. The goal of this chapter is to explore that zone of control, even knowing this will be a messy trial-and-error process and that there is no one-size-fits-all strategy that is sure to work.

The first step is to start from where you are.

Where are you now with your mood? You may start off in a difficult place, amid a severe depression, where the zone of control is most limited. In severe depressions, it can be a great struggle to get out of bed, go for a short walk, read, or even do basic hygiene. In severe depressions, a person may turn completely away from the world, canceling all engagements, not answering the phone. But even here in this tightest of spaces, there are things you can try.

If you feel up to it (and even if you aren't), I invite you to experiment with your mood. Take a leap of trust:

- Push yourself to take that shower.
- Walk 15 minutes in nature (or just in your neighborhood).
- Call a friend, or make an appointment to get help.
- List five things that you are grateful for.

These are baby steps. But even the smallest baby steps are still steps. With severe depression, each small step amounts to a small win. When you were a baby, you had to crawl before you walked. The same is true for severe depression. And some days may not offer a small win. That's okay too. Don't beat yourself up for having a bad day. If nothing else, congratulate yourself for getting this far. Merely coexisting with severe depression is an achievement.

Identifying and recording the small things you can do each day to move mood may seem primitive, but such humble actions mirror techniques from established depression therapies, such as cognitive–behavioral therapy (CBT). This process of taking inventory of the actions that may change mood and then scheduling future actions is called *behavioral activation*. The good news is that some modest degree of behavioral activation is possible even in the most severe depression. Use it!

You may face a more moderate depression that affords you more room to operate. If you're able to concentrate, you may be able to read and plan a more elaborate program to better your mood. Reading a self-help book may be the first thing we imagine a depressed individual can do for themself. Is it worth the investment of time and energy?

Do self-help books help depression?

Self-help can refer to any program designed for an individual to undertake on their own, with or without a treating professional who might monitor or assist. The advantage of self-help in book form is that books are affordable and accessible and can efficiently propose a structured program for improving mood.

When self-help books are used in a systematic way, scientists term this *bibliotherapy*. The value of bibliotherapy for depression depends on several things, not the least of which is the quality of the book. Picking a random title in the self-help section is not a recipe for success. Most of the books that have been evaluated as bibliotherapy take psychological approaches to depression. The most common approaches feature exercises for achieving cognitive changes (similar to those encouraged in CBT) and/or making behavioral changes to your routine.

Does bibliotherapy work? Based on the research to date, we can give it two cheers. We'd love to give it more, but only a modest amount of research has evaluated unguided bibliotherapy (read without therapist assistance) or guided bibliotherapy (read with therapist assistance). Nevertheless, existing evaluations offer preliminary—but real—evidence that self-help books can aid depression, especially when the depression is mild to moderate. Understandably, the benefits of self-help books may be more elusive for severely depressed persons, for whom reading and following through on complex recommendations is a greater challenge.

This book as an overview of depression. I hope it will offer you some important tools and principles for thinking about and even acting upon your mood, but it does not represent a full-fledged therapeutic program. Indeed, that would be another book! For interested readers who want specific self-help book recommendations, see the resource list at the end of the text. Because let's face it, the genre of self-help can be a minefield. I fear many readers may have already had less than fruitful experiences with self-help books. In a nearly $2 billion industry, it's inevitable that false hopes will be raised and solutions overpromised. But from the great mass of self-help books, have faith that some rise to the level of actual helpfulness.

Self-help books, although not a cure-all, are part of a wider societal strategy to curtail depression. Bearing in mind that depression is undertreated and that people face barriers of cost and access to entering formal treatment, books—because of their low cost and high accessibility—are an important means to boost the number of people who receive help.

As technology evolves, additional avenues to deliver depression self-help will open up, including modalities that will be even more accessible, user-friendly, and (it is hoped) inexpensive. Eventually, books will no longer be the main "delivery system" for self-help.

An avenue that's closest to being ready for "prime time" is internet delivery of self-help psychotherapies. This avenue translates existing psychotherapies into self-paced, self-guided Web-based administration. Again, much like the market for books, the market for self-help on the internet is a Wild West. Indiscriminately consulting websites is not a recipe for success. Again, to help you navigate this Wild West, links to specific vetted websites are offered at the end of the text. (Note that this space is dynamic and future editions of this book will likely feature a different list.) As before, the greatest support exists for internet-based resources that take psychological approaches to depression, specifically CBT and interpersonal psychotherapy. Typically, these websites offer a series of tools that include symptom monitoring, exercises, and workbooks. Costs are low relative to in-person therapy, and in some cases these programs are free. Browse a few to see which is right for you.

No doubt, technological ferment will continue, transforming how self-help is conceived of and delivered. Self-help content will increasingly be offered on computers and on apps that run on a smartphone or tablet. These apps will only proliferate as smartphones remain our portals to the world and as apps are programmed to be engaging, gamelike (with music and graphics), and customized. It is easy to imagine a future in which mental health apps might dominate how depression self-help is delivered. It's even possible to imagine that mental health apps will become so sophisticated with artificial intelligence features that they could simulate and/or compete with psychotherapy. For the moment, however, therapists still have a job. At this point, few available mental health apps have been examined critically, and evaluated apps may not be available for public download. Feel free to explore, just do not expect too much yet. My recommendation is to bookmark depression/mental health apps as something to watch and try during the next 5–10 years.

What about the role of exercise, sleep, or pets?

A main premise of this book is that many factors propel humans into depression. The obverse of this premise also holds: Numerous routes run out of depression. This fact has major implications for mood management at the individual level. Individuals need not commit to any one approach. There are numerous dishes at the mood buffet; these offerings are a la carte—you can sample some, or all of them, at your discretion. In this section, I consider some of the most sustaining, most supported ways to bend mood in a positive direction.

Exercise may be one of the most underrated antidepressants. A major review of 39 randomized trials for people with clinical depression compared exercise with either no treatment or an established treatment (e.g., talk therapy). Overall, the evidence indicates that exercise improves the symptoms of depression. At the same time, questions remain about exactly how strong the benefits of exercise are, what are the best types of exercise, and how long the benefits last. Some evidence suggests that exercise probably needs to be continued over the longer term to maintain the benefits on mood. All things being equal, choose exercise activities that you enjoy doing (walking, skiing, tennis, or whatever it might be). One 2016 review reported that larger antidepressant effects were found for moderate-intensity, aerobic exercise, as well as when activities were supervised by exercise professionals.

The bottom line is that engaging in regular exercise is likely to benefit your mood. Based on today's research, we can't state whether exercise is more or less effective than drug-based or psychologically based therapies. We just know that exercise is a good tool for moving mood. Use it if you can.

Exercise is a good tool in part because it is a great complement to other mood-restoring measures. Perhaps the best illustration is how exercise can complement efforts to improve a sleep routine (exercising during the day improves the odds that one will be able to fall asleep at night). Improving sleep is a key avenue for improving mood because poor sleep is one of the most destructive forces for mood. Night after night, when people sleep poorly, sleep problems come to loom over waking hours: Imagine starting the day already exhausted, demoralized by negative thoughts, and unable to cope with the day's challenges. Unfortunately, people's default responses to sleep problems can make the situation worse. For instance, plying yourself with sleeping pills or alcohol may help for a few nights, but it's not a long-term solution for sleep or for mood.

Fortunately, non-drug approaches to poor sleep are increasingly viewed as effective for managing both sleep and related mood problems. If you have the time and the money to work with a specialist trained in CBT for insomnia, this can be a good investment. If not, a do-it-yourself approach to sleep problems is also viable because many of the therapeutic techniques in CBT for insomnia are low-tech and can be performed by a motivated layperson.

The following are the top CBT-type recommendations to get a better night's sleep (notice that this list includes regular exercise):

- Routine! Go to bed at the same time every night, and wake up at the same time every morning.

- Eliminate alcohol, nicotine, and caffeine (and other stimulants) before bedtime.
- Reduce or eliminate napping.
- Use clean sheets and bedding.
- Take a hot shower before bed (you fall asleep as your body cools).
- Do more exercise.
- Bed is for sleep. Avoid working or studying in bed.
- Do not eat or drink before bed (can cause arousal by stimulating digestion and bladder).
- Set aside a daily "worrying time" so worry is not saved for right before bed.
- Control the sleeping environment (comfortable temperature, make it quiet, and make it dark).

For more information about CBT for insomnia, visit the website of the National Sleep Foundation (https://www.thensf. org).

The process of domesticating a variety of animals has taken place over many millennia; we have kept dogs and cats as pets for approximately 10,000 years. Clearly, there must be something in it for humans! Pet owners the world over will swear upon the emotional bonds forged with their furry friends. There is surprisingly little systematic knowledge about pet interactions and depression, in part because high-quality studies are difficult to perform. But some suggestive evidence exists. We have reason to believe that interactions with pets may have mood-lifting properties:

- Pet ownership teaches us compassion and a sense of responsibility. We know our pets are helpless and must depend on us for food, shelter, and water. Owning a pet shows us we can care for another living thing when we might otherwise feel totally incompetent. Gardening or caring for a plant makes a similar demonstration. That alone can give us a reason to live.

- Decreasing stress: Pets are physical creatures. It can be soothing to cuddle with a cat or dog. It distracts us from negative thoughts and feelings.
- Pets help us feel less alone. Dogs can provide constant, unconditional love. They accept us for who we are when we might feel judged by other humans. And they're just plain cute and act in silly ways.
- Relatedly, pets can provide easier opportunities to socialize, such as by meeting people who want to interact with our pets. This is important because depression is so isolating.
- Owning a pet encourages us to exercise (which, as noted previously, is beneficial for mood). Taking a dog on a regular walk gets us moving, may help us collect our thoughts, and may provide structure and routine when we're feeling unmoored.

It's okay if you love dogs or cats but can't commit to or afford one right now. Consider trying pet sitting or even borrowing a friend's animal. A smaller commitment to care for other organisms such as fish or plants may also help mood by the same principles.

How can I discover my secret weapon against depression?

There is a simple bottom line: You have to be willing to experiment. We already considered some helpful strategies for moving mood in the right direction. To identify all potential candidates, it is necessary to reach beyond what is known with complete certainty. For example, there are techniques and practices that have been endorsed by basic research as useful for mood but have not yet been carefully evaluated in people struggling with clinical depression. If you're depressed and feeling out of options, you can't wait 15 years for fully conclusive research. So I ask you to consider a broader array of tools, among which you might find your secret weapon against depression. The costs of exploring these tools are relatively low, and the possible benefits are high. There is only one way to find out which works best for you!

There are two families of actions you might consider. The first family involves taking steps to initiate a more loving inner dialogue. Let's call this family *talking the talk*. These steps are so important because depression gives a person's inner critic a huge megaphone. Part and parcel of a strong negative mood is to flood the sufferer with mood-congruent thoughts and interpretations. The mood machine becomes adept at blasting the sufferer with the harshest of words. Classics are "You're a failure!" "No one loves you!" You are going to die alone!" and "No one will miss you when you're gone!" When castigated in this way, it's natural to react with further upset. And many sufferers do.

This is why it is vital to consider self-management techniques that help you dial down the volume on this inner critic. Before a brighter (or saner) inner conversation may take place, you must quiet the critic. This process takes time and requires patience and persistence.

One simple first step is recognizing that the steady stream of criticism issuing from the self may be a strong mood talking. The inner critic does not speak from a place of absolute truth. A second step is using specific techniques that allow you to begin to calm the mind. Specifically, some people may find value in meditation-type practices.

Meditation may sound like an enormous commitment. But you do not need to become a full-on yogi to reap its benefits. Meditation practices are worth trying because they are simple and low cost. These practices require no more than a few spare minutes and a quiet place. There you can engage in exercises in which you focus on your breathing and on the sensations that are passing through your body. There are many guided meditations that can be explored for free on social media channels, such as YouTube. Through a regular meditation practice, you may find that you are better able to control your attention and still your mind when it brims over with upsetting thoughts. One book that could help you get started is Chade-Meng Tan's *Joy on Demand* (HarperCollins, 2016), which includes mediation practices that are as brief as 15 seconds.

One specific type of meditation technique that has some supportive evidence behind it is mindfulness meditation. Mindfulness mediation appears particularly helpful for de-escalating depressive feelings. Mindfulness mediation features a set of techniques that teaches a person to become more invested in the present moment rather than being consumed with the failures of the past or the anxieties of the future. While present focused, you also become a more neutral observer of the contents of your mind. Many mindfulness exercises teach you to resist the urge to judge or react to what your mind is saying. Normally, we tend to label or judge physical feelings or thoughts as "bad" or "good" thoughts. Instead, this meditation practice focuses on acknowledging or accepting one's thoughts and feelings. With practice, it becomes possible to reduce your emotional reactivity to your thought stream and, by extension, your inner critic. For those interested in learning more about mindfulness meditation, a classic book on the topic is Mark Williams et al.'s *The Mindful Way Through Depression: Freeing Yourself from Chronic Unhappiness* (Guilford, 2007).

Working on your mental dialogue is not only a matter of trying to turn down the volume on the inner critic but also a matter of turning up the volume on a kinder inner voice. There are several ways to begin a more loving inner dialogue. A first step is simply committing yourself to a better relationship with yourself. After all, most depressed people spend considerable time working on relationships with friends, family members, and co-workers; what about your relationship with yourself, which may be the most important one of all? Many people who struggle with depression notice that they say things to themselves that they would never say to a friend or a family member. It can be helpful to ask yourself what it would sound like inside if you cared for yourself. Can you begin to talk to yourself that way? Change is difficult, of course. Recognize that many other people have faced this exact challenge during a mood disorder and come out the other side. Knowing that you aren't alone can help reframe your struggle in a more positive way. Entertain the thought that a person like you, someone who has struggled through months or years of depression—like you—maybe deserves a little more patience and even kindness. You used to think, "I'm a failure" or "I'm broken." Now think, "I've survived a lot and have the bumps and bruises to prove it." It takes active work to talk to yourself in a kinder way—but it is worth the effort!

Learning to listen differently to the inner critic and cultivating a kinder inner voice are important vehicles for mood improvement. A second family of actions that complement this theme of talking the talk of self-love we might call *walking the walk.*

After all, it only makes sense to take new actions that are consistent with intentional self-love, and taking actions that show that you respect yourself and your body and prioritize your needs can be a powerful wellspring of mood. Such actions can not only bolster your newfound inner voice but also may serve to correct or challenge a whole host of self-harming and self-hating actions that build up during depression—from neglecting hygiene to self-injury and denying yourself simple pleasures. What can you do to demonstrate that you care about your mind and body?

Everyone's loving actions may be slightly different. Self-loving actions may include both things we have discussed and new items:

- Getting enough sleep
- Eating a healthier diet
- Cutting back on alcohol and drugs
- Taking the time/making the time to exercise
- Giving yourself space for fun or reflection, especially if I you are stressed (and allowing yourself to take a break from the news or social media)

- Taking time to appreciate your friends and enjoy other people
- Spending time with the people who really love you
- Standing up for yourself if someone tried to take advantage of you
- Keeping a gratitude journal (in which every day you write down four or five things you are grateful for)

The overall take-home message of this chapter is that there is no "right way" to help yourself—and no wrong way. It is okay to improvise. It is okay to learn over time about what works best for you. You can mix and match. And you can combine any of these recommendations with formal therapies. What is most important is to keep trying, to keep learning what works best for you, and to apply what you learn consistently so you can eventually fully recover from depression and remain healthy afterward.

13

HOW TO TALK ABOUT DEPRESSION AND HELP A DEPRESSED PERSON

Why is depression so difficult to talk about?

It's the third decade of the 21st century and depression is still difficult to talk about. Why?

There are three interrelated reasons. First, unlike physical health problems such as cancer or a broken leg, there are no physical proofs of depression—the sufferer can't pull out an X-ray to explain their pain. Because depression's wounds aren't visible, some may doubt if it is a "legitimate" reason to suffer. If you haven't experienced it yourself, it requires imagination to understand a depressed person's predicament.

Second, because mental health conditions are scary and poorly understood, they are often demonized. For example, after many mass shootings, there's often a rush to attribute vicious homicidal behavior to mental illnesses such as depression. (This is ironic because people with mental illness are more likely to be victims of homicide than the average person in the general population.) Repeated suggestions that the mentally ill are dangerous and unpredictable naturally breed further fear and fan the tendency for people to shy away from interaction with a depressed person.

Third, we lack good scripts for social interaction around mental health problems. Consequently, a conspiracy of silence often builds up around the depressed person. Depressed people themselves are part of the conspiracy; depressed people feel worthless, like they are no good, and so they are inclined to hide themselves, withdraw, and not discuss their problems. The people who surround the depressed person also join the conspiracy. Often, people don't know what to say or how to act around the depressed person. Fearing they will say or do "the wrong thing" may leave them not saying or doing anything. Caregivers are particularly likely to keep their struggles to themselves; they perceive (accurately) that others in their social network don't want to hear about depression. They fear embarrassing conversations, the loss of friends, and becoming the subject of gossip and whisper. So they remain isolated in their support role. Again, the contrast to physical illness is striking. When a cancer diagnosis is announced, scripts launch people into action to help the afflicted and their support network: meals, cleaning, childcare, monetary support, whatever you need! With depression, a new diagnosis is rarely announced—itself telling—and the response of others is far less coordinated.

Obviously, the only way to break this conspiracy of silence and bring depression out of the shadows is to talk about depression more openly and honestly. Talking about depression is certainly not easy, but it is well worth doing. Depressed people would benefit: It's easier to manage the symptoms of depression if one is not a social outcast at the same time. Exhausted caregivers would benefit. Most people feel lighter after sharing their burden. And what a relief to not have to continue the charade of putting on a false face or pretending everything is okay!

Breaking down conversation barriers

Jack was feeling isolated and depressed. He was a proud man, so when he started to struggle, he didn't want to admit that he might be depressed. For weeks, he didn't want to admit it even to himself. As he considered what to do, he didn't know where to start or whom to talk to first. Jack was unsure about talking to friends or family, so he thought it would help to start with a more neutral person. Indeed, if you're hesitant to start with your close relations, you might begin with a doctor or a counselor, teacher, or spiritual advisor. The important thing is to talk to someone you trust about how you feel—just saying it out loud might give you some relief. Indeed, Jack felt better after talking to his doctor. He now knew it was depression and had a plan for dealing with it.

Make no mistake. Talking about depression isn't easy. Know there is no such thing as a perfect conversation. When Jack first brought up his depression to his girlfriend, Samantha, he was very nervous. He put off the conversation a half dozen times. Only after he had jotted down all the main points that he wanted to explain, was we finally ready to start the conversation. Ironically, sometimes talking with the people closest to you is the most difficult of all. The following are ideas for first words in a conversation with a friend or family member:

- "I think something's wrong because I feel _____. I'm worried that I may be depressed. Can we talk?"
- "I want to talk to you about something that's hard for me to put into words. I feel _____, and it's been going on for a while now."
- "Even though I may seem fine on the outside, I feel _____ on the inside."

Jack's initial talk with his girlfriend went well. Samantha did not run away after he mentioned how he'd been feeling these past few weeks leading up to his doctor's visit. She knew that something was wrong when Jack had canceled their date twice in a row. and now she knew why. Now 3 weeks into his treatment, Jack faced another common conversation challenge—asking for help. He believed that asking for help would make him feel too vulnerable, and the depression already made him feel insecure, like he had to "swallow his pride." Jack's doctor reminded Jack that just living with depression is by itself a great challenge. Dr. Shaw pointed out, "You wouldn't hesitate to ask for help if you had cancer or a broken leg. Why was depression any different?" The doctor helped Jack come up with the right way to put it: "Samantha, I may need extra support while I'm struggling." Indeed, when you're asking for support, be as specific as you can. You can even say, "You can support me by _____. That would be really helpful to me." For example, if you need help connecting with a therapist, ask for support to make or keep an appointment. Sometimes, people will be able to help you in the ways you need. Sometimes, they will not. Your best bet, however, is to give your support team a chance by clearly communicating your needs.

Conversations about depression are of course a two-way street. We also need to break down the barriers that prevent caregivers or friends from having conversations about depression. Jack's best friend, Frank, had noticed that Jack seemed preoccupied and touchy. When their friend group went to the diner, Jack didn't participate in any of their usual ribbing. Jack also didn't touch his food, and it looked like he had lost weight. It was all very out of character, but Frank didn't know how to bring it up. When you're concerned one of your close relations might be depressed, starting a conversation is the best way for you to understand the seriousness of the situation, open a dialogue, and determine if you can help. It's okay if you feel nervous. Try to speak calmly and with a reassuring tone. Tell the person that you're concerned about them and that you're there to help. If it's not an emergency, you can say "I'm here whenever you're ready."

The following are tips for starting a conversation with a person you're concerned about:

- Find a private place to talk.
- Let your loved one talk about how they feel.
- Tell them you care about them. Say things such as "I'm here," "I care," "I want to help," and "How can I help?"

- Ask directly if they're thinking about suicide.
- Try your hardest not to judge what you hear. Don't tell them that their feelings are wrong or bad.
- Resist the urge to try to solve or downplay the person's problems.
- Do your best not to take your loved one's actions or hurtful words personally.
- Use body language to signal that you are fully present. Eye contact and leaning forward are signs that you're listening.

It is important to be clear about the goals of depression conversations. I have underscored the value of talking to a depressed person to keep lines of communication open and to indicate support. But let's face it, many people want something else when they speak to a depressed person: to fix the person. Naturally, no one likes to see suffering and everyone wants the depressed person to "get back to normal," so it's tempting to launch a "fixing" conversation in which you offer advice or even ask the depressed person to change. While understandable, "fixing" conversations often go poorly. It's important to understand why these conversations fail.

First, experience proves that it is not possible to "talk the person out of their depression." Telling the depressed person they "have a good life," "other people have it worse," or that the person has "no reason to be depressed" does not make the depression vanish. Worse, such statements risk creating an interpersonal rift. When you say or imply that a person's depression lacks a valid reason, the other person will almost inevitably feel belittled. The truth is that depression does not always make sense or even need a reason. Relatedly, fixing advice such as "just think positive," "cheer up," or "have you considered yoga?" tends to trivialize the difficulty of depression. Obviously, if depression could be vanquished through such simple steps, it wouldn't exist at all. There is also the danger that well-meaning statements such as these will be experienced as blaming because they imply the depressed person is depressed because he or she failed to do something.

So, to emphasize, you are more likely to be successful in your conversation with a depressed person if you remember that your primary goal is to listen and support rather than to fix. The following are statements you can say in support conversations:

- "I can relate."
- "You're not alone."
- "How have you been lately?"
- "I want you to know that you are important to me."
- "Thank you for sharing!"
- "This took a lot of courage to share, and I'm glad you did."
- "A lot of what you shared resonates with me. Thank you."
- "I'm here if you need to talk."
- "Is there anything I can do to help?"
- "I love you" or "I care about you."
- (If they aren't in treatment) "Depression can be treated successfully. It is something you'd consider?"

In support conversations, it can also help the depressed person if you provide gentle reminders of hope. You don't need to go overboard, and the person won't believe you if you promise everything will be better tomorrow. But you can say, "I believe you will get better" or "I will never give up on you." In support conversations, it can also be very helpful to remind the depressed person about their strengths, which they often lose sight of. When pointing out strengths, it often helps if you can recall specific accomplishments.

What else can you do to help a friend or family member who is depressed?

One of the most loving things you can do for a depressed person is listen in support conversations. Listening is hard work, so never underestimate the value of offering a listening ear. But there are other things day to day that you can do to make yourself a stronger ally.

Frank had lost a family member to suicide, so he was determined that he would do everything he could to support Jack. Sometimes, he would give Jack a quick phone call or send a text to check in on him. When Jack was really struggling, Frank would offer to run errands for him or to come over to help Jack make progress on the routine tasks that had piled up—the dirty laundry and the dishes that had stacked up in the sink. He understood that Jack wouldn't always be up for company, but Frank always felt better after checking in on his buddy.

Samantha also learned how to become a stronger ally. She learned more about depression and its treatment (by reading books such as this). She decided the best thing she could do would be to help Jack find a good therapist (in addition to the doctor who had prescribed medications). She learned that depressed people need a lot of encouragement to start and stay in therapy, as well as staying the course of a medication treatment when it doesn't immediately work. She helped Jack gather information about possible therapists and helped him organize his questions or thoughts before the first meeting.

Helping a person through depression is more likely to be a marathon than a sprint. You have to pace yourself. One reason why Jack got through his depression is that Samantha and Frank talked regularly and compared notes about how to best help Jack. In fact, they developed a system in which they "took turns," so the burdens of giving Jack extra help and support were shared on different days. This underscores a critical point: You can't help the depressed person if you are totally burned out. Neglecting your own care ultimately hurts everyone. Make sure you are getting enough sleep and exercise and that you are eating okay. Make sure you dedicate time to recharge. It is also okay to set limits on how and when you can be a support. When setting a limit, be explicit. For example, you might say, "I can't talk until ____. Can I check in with you then?"

When depression becomes a crisis

It can be difficult to see a loved one struggle with depression, even when depression is managed. But there can be times when, despite best efforts, depression spirals and turns into a crisis.

Depression is always serious. So, what's a *crisis*?

A crisis is whenever someone with a mental health problem like depression is at risk of hurting themselves or someone else. How do you know? There are a few signs that someone might be in crisis. Someone might talk about the following:

- Unbearable pain
- Feeling trapped
- Having no reason to live
- Killing or hurting themselves or another person. They might make statements such as "after I'm gone."
- Feeling totally hopeless. They might make statements such as "I can't take it anymore."

The following behaviors can signal a crisis:

- Major changes in alcohol or drug use
- Looking for ways to hurt themselves, such as researching or buying a gun
- Suddenly withdrawing from other people and activities
- Giving away important possessions
- Calling people to say goodbye
- Sleeping too much or too little
- Acting aggressively or recklessly
- Acting with rage, irritability, or shame

It can be scary to take the first step if someone you love is going through a mental health crisis. It's okay if you feel nervous. Try to speak calmly and with a reassuring tone. It's understandable if you feel like you don't have all the answers (because you don't). But you're not completely powerless either. You can help with a constructive response. Tell the person that you're concerned for their well-being and that you're there to help. Don't assume that others will step up and that you can wait for them to do it. Remember that by connecting a person in crisis to the help they need, you can save a life.

Call for help immediately if you think a person is at risk of hurting themselves or another person. Take what they're telling you seriously. Stay with the person. If you can, remove any means of potential harm. Call for help and consider escorting them to an emergency room if necessary.

You don't have to handle a crisis alone. The following resources can help:

- Call 911 in the case of a life-threatening emergency. Tell the operator that it's a psychiatric emergency. Ask for an officer who's trained to assist people in a psychiatric emergency.
- The National Suicide Prevention Lifeline provides free and confidential support over the phone to people in distress as well as crisis resources for loved ones and professionals. Call 800-273-8255 to speak with a trained crisis counselor.
- The Crisis Text Line is a 24-hour service that provides crisis resources via text messages. Text HOME to 741741 to help the person connect with a trained crisis counselor to receive crisis support via text message.
- The National Domestic Violence Hotline is a 24-hour service that provides crisis resources to anyone experiencing domestic violence or seeking resources and information on the topic. Call 800-799-7233 to speak with trained experts who provide confidential support.
- The National Sexual Assault Hotline is a 24-hour service that provides crisis resources to people affected by sexual violence. Call 800-656-4673 to connect with a trained staff member in your area.

PART IV

LIFE AFTER DEPRESSION

14

WHAT IS THE LONG-TERM PROGNOSIS FOR DEPRESSION?

Peering into the future

Everyone wants to know what the future holds. That's why there will always be a market for horoscopes and fortune tellers. If you've struggled with depression, that desire to know the future takes on greater urgency. Unfortunately, depressed people do not receive the most balanced information about their likely prognosis. Whether in scientific articles, popular accounts, or conversations in the consulting room, the bleak prospects get featured. There are many different variants of bad outcome: further episodes, increased chance of self-harm, death by suicide, hospitalization, and drug overdoses.

No question, bad prospects form part of depression's sobering reality. We've laid out the evidence that depression recurs for approximately half of sufferers, with harms that often compound over time. But scientific authorities present these harms as a done deal. A representative example is presented by Saba Moussavi and colleagues from the World Health Organization in the medical journal, *The Lancet*: "Without treatment, depression has the tendency to assume a chronic course, be recurrent, and over time to be associated with increasing disability." The unavoidable impression from reading much of the scientific literature is that if you've had depression once, it will probably strike you down again and lay waste to your good years. You'll be impaired at work, your relationships will suffer, and your happiness and sense of meaning in life will be obstructed. Although this perspective captures some of the reality of depression diagnosis for some people, it is also incomplete and even misleading.

The most obvious problem with the bleak conventional wisdom about prognosis is that it glosses over approximately half of depressed people—the size of the group that does not experience recurrence. As it turns out, non-recurrent depression has been radically understudied. As psychologists Scott Monroe and Kate Harkness state, "These people constitute approximately one-half of the population of depressed persons and represent the most important and promising group for future study. Yet they have been essentially ignored." Obviously, what is not studied cannot be counted. Instead, the database of depression is founded on samples of depressed people who are either seen in treatment settings such as university psychiatry departments or who decide to volunteer for research. In both of these cases, the samples inevitably skew toward persons who have been depressed repeatedly and/or chronically.

One puzzle is why people with a single, well-resolved lifetime episode of depression are less likely to participate in research. Maybe because these people have struggled less with the condition, they consequently find the label "depression" to be less salient to their identity; it is even possible that they may decline participation in a depression study because they wish to avoid any reminders of depression. Some of the fault may lie with researchers; it requires extra resources to systematically recruit this group, and with time, money, and effort being finite, it hasn't been a priority.

We know for certain that people with single episodes of depression exist. The few longitudinal studies that use large and representative samples of the population consistently find that 40–60% of people who have had depression once never experience a recurrence, even years or decades later. In other words, it is as about as common for depression to be a one-time life event as it is for depression to be repeated. Yet the actual lives of those who have a single lifetime depression episode remain largely a mystery. This omission not only warps our picture of depression prognosis but also obstructs our ability to learn why different people have different prognoses and specifically why some have only a single episode of depression, whereas others have depression that recurs. Indeed, careful study of single-episode depression may hold important clues or lessons about how to prevent recurrent depression.

Ignoring the reality of good outcomes has another untoward effect. Talking about the future and omitting the good outcomes when you speak to depressed people will only lower the morale of a group that already struggles with its morale. To the extent that mental health professionals downplay good outcomes, they send an implicit message to depressed people: "Do not aim too high."

The standard treatment guidelines for depression (guidance that informs what mental health professionals do and say to their patients) likewise have the effect of reinforcing the "aim low" message. The main goals set by these guidelines are to reduce the symptoms of depression and limit the number of future episodes. Depression is approached as a lifelong condition in which depression symptoms must be continuously monitored and managed. In other words, these guidelines set the main goal for patients to be less bothered by depression. Although having fewer symptoms is undoubtedly a good thing, it is strange and slightly jarring that a higher aspiration—of a positive state of mental health—goes unmentioned. Patients express this higher aspiration on surveys about their hopes for treatment: A strong majority endorses health goals such as feelings of well-being, satisfying relationships, or good functioning on the job.

The neglect of positive outcomes is also evident when we compare popular dialogue about the possibility of recovery after depression to the dialogue regarding recovery after other significant mental health conditions. Consider alcoholism, for example. With drinking problems, there are intense dialogues around the concept of recovery, about what recovery entails, about what the stages of recovery are, and about how recovery can be maintained. For substance problems, there is even an organized recovery movement. Virtually everyone in the United States has heard of popular 12-step programs such as Alcoholics Anonymous, which are among the entities centered around facilitating people's transition from drinking to a better mental and spiritual place. For depression, the corresponding recovery movement is weaker, more diffuse, and less organized.

Given that adverse outcomes after depression have been so heavily emphasized, this chapter aims for balance. Specifically, to provide the most comprehensive and accurate picture of depression prognosis requires fleshing out terms such as recovery and also assembling what is known about good outcomes. That is the present mission.

What is meant by terms such as recovery, response, or remission?

Just when Joe thought he would be stuck in a chronic depression forever, he started to get better. He wasn't sure why it happened. Did the birth of his daughter a year ago stir in him reasons to live? Did a string of work successes renew his self-confidence? Was it the sessions with his therapist, which gave him new insights about his low mood and how to cope with it? Was it trail running, which started as a weekend hobby and then blossomed into a true passion and way to relieve daily stress? Whatever the reason, or reasons, slowly, but surely, Joe improved. Gradually he became functional, not only in his job but also in his relationships and his ability to give back to his community (he was a Little League baseball coach). As Joe's symptoms of depression inexorably waned, he gradually regained his health and happiness. It was clear Joe was better, but was he all better? When is it correct to say that he, or anyone else, has recovered from depression?

Over time, the mental health field has developed clear criteria for determining when depression is present, and clinicians are good at assessing people for a diagnosis. By contrast, the criteria for declaring when depression is gone are not nearly as established; correspondingly, clinicians and researchers are not as adept at assessing recovery. In the past 20 years, researchers have begun to develop more concrete definitions of these concepts, as well as some helpful rules of thumb for measuring good outcomes. Let's apply these to mark key milestones on Joe's upward trajectory from response to remission to recovery.

For example, in the world of treatment, a first convention for noting improvement is that of a response. For Joe, the moment of response was the week when he first showed a greater than 50% improvement in symptoms and no longer met the criteria for a depression diagnosis. Notably, at this point, Joe was at once better and also far from well. Even improved, he still labored with depression symptoms, such as disturbed sleep and fatigue. Joe was able to do his work, but it still required more energy than usual to concentrate. Overall, in this state Joe still felt like he was "treading water."

The next key moment, remission, marked an even more dramatic change. At this point, Joe no longer had any appreciable symptoms of depression as carefully assessed by a clinician. The lack of symptoms is the key requirement for declaring a person remitted from depression. At the moment of remission, Joe finally believed that he had returned to his normal self. This normality felt tentative at first, and Joe was naturally fearful that it would not last.

This brings us, finally, to the notion of recovery, which is an even higher bar to clear than remission. Although there is no single definition of recovery, the most accepted and rigorous one requires a person's symptoms to remain negligible or entirely absent for a sustained period of time. Applied to Joe's case, it means remaining essentially symptom-free for 8 consecutive weeks. When Joe reached the point of recovery, he was now seeing depression in the rearview mirror, as a past chapter of his life. Interestingly, a major study of 431 psychiatric patients who were followed for more than 12 years found that in 41% of the almost 196,000 follow-up weeks, patients were asymptomatic. A totally asymptomatic state is relatively common in the natural history of depression, again somewhat belying the idea that depression is invariably a chronic condition.

Response, remission, and recovery are more than just academic terminology. They are milestones that help us predict what will happen next to a person. Most strikingly, when people such as Joe meet the stringent criteria for recovery, this foretells that more long-lasting positive outcomes are likely to continue. Longitudinal studies document that recovering and meeting a 2-month asymptomatic status signals that sustained relief from depression, potentially even for years, is much more likely to ensue.

The flip side of this proposition is that not meeting the recovery standard bodes ill. Research has shown that the presence of residual depression symptoms predicts surprisingly poor outcomes. This is concerning because residual symptoms such as lingering difficulties with sleep and fatigue are incredibly common. Yet even relatively minor residual symptoms predict worse outcomes across a variety of metrics, including a return of a full episode of depression, a worse course of other mental health conditions, increased use of medical services, and increased risk of suicide and substance problems. Minor symptoms are also predict worse functioning in other key domains, including functioning on the job, in the family, and in important relationships. One important question for future work is why minor symptoms have major effects over time. These findings underscore the clinical importance of meeting the full recovery standard.

Despite the clear value of a sustained symptom-free outcome, or recovery, most clinical studies and intervention studies (drugs or psychotherapy) continue to focus on whether patients respond or improve. Waiting until participants fully recover is almost certainly more time-consuming (and likely more costly and labor-intensive) than studying response or even remission. From a more cynical perspective, if recovery were the focus, studied interventions would not perform as well because many fewer persons would be able to meet the recovery endpoints. In any event, because full recovery from depression is not routinely included as an outcome, we don't know as much about it as we should.

How common is full recovery from depression (and what explains why it happens)?

The overwhelming majority of people who have an episode of depression will make a full recovery. However, estimates of how common it is for depressed people to fully recover and how quickly recovery occurs are imprecise. Studies can vary with regard to what kinds of depressed people are enrolled, duration of the follow-up period, and the exact details that are used to establish recovery. Standard research designs, including ones in my laboratory, often underestimate full recovery from depression. This is because they employ volunteer samples of depressed people or sample patients who are in treatment for depression, which disproportionately represent people with severe and/or chronic depression (who are slower to recover). In one of my studies, for instance, only one in five depressed patients met stringent full-recovery criteria at a 6-month follow-up. More hopeful, a landmark investigation led by Martin Keller found that 50% of a large group of depressed patients had recovered by 6-month follow-up. A major review of work in this area concludes that more than half and up to 70% of patients will recover if the follow-up is extended to 1 year. Obviously, with longer follow-up periods, a higher percentage of patients will fully recover. However, studies with the longest follow-up periods offer a caveat: When a depressed person has not recovered by 1 year, the chances for recovery diminish in subsequent months.

In studies that use more representative samples of depressed people, full recovery occurs faster and more reliably. For example, a study of an adult population in the Netherlands found that 50% of depressed people had recovered in 3 months' time. This percentage matched that of an investigation of Japanese patients who were in their first episode of depression and who took on average 3 months after initiation of treatment to recover. In summary, in the community, recovery from depression appears to occur faster and be more complete than recovery in clinical patient samples.

What predicts full recovery from depression? At this point, we have enough data to support reasonable hunches about who is more likely to achieve full recovery. It is fair to say that full recovery is more likely in people who have

- less severe depression;
- depressions that are not already chronic;
- few co-occurring physical and mental health conditions;
- a high level of previous functioning; and
- high levels of social support.

Can people flourish after depression?

Six months after his depression ended, Joe compared himself to the person he was before depression and he noticed several positive changes. After depression, Joe was more patient, less likely to be irritated by the little things, more grateful for what he had, kinder, and maybe even happier. Recovery by itself is certainly wonderful to contemplate, but Joe's experience raises the question of whether depression is ever a bridge to something better. It happens at least sometimes. For example, celebrities such as Kristen Bell have given eloquent accounts of depression struggles that paved the way to a dramatically improved life. But is there more systematic evidence that people thrive after depression?

Some evidence is in hand. My laboratory has been among the first to document the phenomenon of high functioning after depression. As a first step, we have focused on psychological well-being—investigating whether some depressed persons go on to experience high levels of well-being, or what we call optimal well-being (OWB). We focused on psychological well-being for three reasons: (1) Well-being is a key aspiration of depressed people (people want to lead happy, fulfilling lives with meaningful relationships); (2) well-being data have been shown previously to be predictive of depression prognosis, over and above measures of symptoms (initial work shows people with higher levels of well-being are protected against future depression and anxiety); and (3) well-being is fairly easy to study and can be readily measured.

Good science requires clear and consistent definitions, and this is certainly true for a concept such as OWB, which could mean several different things. Our standard for OWB after depression is a high bar that has three elements. First, we require the person to have recovered from depression. Second, the previously depressed person needs to report objectively high levels of psychological well-being, which we set as better than 75% of nondepressed adult peers (based on standardized norms). Third, where workable, we also include measures of disability and require that the person report objectively low levels of disability.

Can depressed people ever hope to reach this lofty standard? Our work indicates that they can do so. Our first study used a representative sample of 3,487 adults from the Midlife in the United States study. We found that nearly 10% of the people who had a depression diagnosis at the initial assessment reported OWB 10 years later. As a point of comparison, only approximately 20 of nondepressed participants met the same well-being criterion. Far from negating the possibility of achieving OWB, depression only reduced a person's chance of achieving it by half. Because there is no fully agreed upon OWB standard, some might say our standard for OWB was too restrictive. If so, our study data are even more hopeful: With a looser OWB standard, more than 10% of previously depressed persons would be enjoying optimal well-being.

Adding to our confidence, we observed a similar pattern in Canada: Approximately 1 in 10 Canadian adults with a history of depression achieved OWB and were approximately half as likely to achieve OWB than nonpsychiatric peers. Interestingly, the prevalence of OWB was higher for people with a history of unipolar depression than it was for people with a history of bipolar mood disorders. Mirroring patterns seen in depression recovery findings, OWB was less common in people who had a history of multiple mental health conditions than it was in persons who had a history of only a single mental health condition.

So we are learning that depression hinders people from achieving OWB but also that the hindrance is less than one might expect. A substantial segment of depressed people appear reborn after depression.

Of course, the complete story of this rebirth has yet to be written. We want to know the full who, how, and why. It is plausible that people can take many different routes to reach this place. For some, full healing may simply require the passage of time. Others may achieve it following formal treatment. Still others may discover a new purpose in life or a daily routine that works for them. Some people may achieve this state after the first time they were depressed; others may achieve it only after several bouts of depression. One motivation to continue this research is that we may discover paths that work through malleable behaviors—behaviors that people can learn or change, such as coping strategies or ways of thinking. If this is the case, it may be possible to teach these behaviors and increase the number of people who achieve OWB after depression.

Finally, one intriguing possibility is that, as we saw with Joe, the experience of depression may open up new pathways to positive development. Although such ideas may be new to depression research, it is increasingly recognized elsewhere that people may grow through pain. Perhaps most explicitly in the field of trauma is the concept of post-traumatic growth, where it has been documented that a sizeable percentage of people who survive a horrible incident will report a greater sense of personal strength or appreciation of life than before the event. A key question for depression research and treatment is how we can help people take away benefits from their unfortunate experience of depression—benefits that leave them in a better position to live their lives after depression.

Knowing now that depression can lead to both good and bad outcomes, in the next chapter we reflect more deeply about living a good life after depression. This includes how people might think about the experience of depression once it has passed, how people might achieve growth in the wake of depression, as well as what people can do to avoid depression's return and what to do if depression starts to return.

15

LIFE AFTER DEPRESSION

The first day of the rest of your life

"What now?" Lonnie was depressed for so long, she forgot what normal was. She forgot what a good day felt like; she even forgot what her old personality was like. After more than 3 years of struggle, she was certain depression was forever, whether that meant she died by suicide or she just died depressed. After 6 more months in a sort of limbo between depression and wellness, Lonnie slowly but surely turned the corner; a year later, her recovery had taken full root.

"What now?" Being better was a gift, although better was also confusing. Lonnie knew the script for being a depressed person. She had less practice at the role of a well person. Everything felt uncertain. How much stress could she take on? What did it mean when, inevitably, she had a bad day? Were these bad feelings depression coming back or was it just a bad day, and how could anyone tell the difference? Wellness also scrambled her relationship rules. As she climbed out of depression, Lonnie found new love. In a bold move, she got engaged to Jonah. Was Jonah Lonnie's savior? They joked about it, and he even got the nickname Saint Jonah. But underneath their levity lurked serious concern. Lonnie worried, "Can I stand on my own feet without him?" Their fights, too, became entangled with Lonnie's depression. Almost inevitably, her bad behaviors—such as passivity and pessimism—would be either blamed on her depression or excused by it. It was like depression was Lonnie's jealous ex, a spurned lover that might show up at any moment and cause a scene.

Making sense of depression after it passes

Most books on depression, this one included, provide tools to fight depression and depressed mood. But what is one to do once depression has passed? Books—reflecting our database—give this topic short shrift.

Less is known about maintaining wellness than about how to combat depression in the first place. Perhaps this is as it should be. After all, people in the middle of depression are most in crisis and need help the most. In addition, much of the advice for "after" depression would overlap with the advice for "during" depression. Consistent with our premise, mood can change for many reasons, meaning that the depression sufferer has multiple points to expand leverage over mood. Critically, these same leverage points are still available after depression has passed. So, even if we have less research than we would like about "after depression," most guidance about how to manage a depressed mood carries over.

To maintain gains after depression, there is support for

- regular exercise;
- good sleep hygiene;
- continuing to curb negative thought patterns;
- maintaining the health of social bonds; and
- availing yourself of therapy (whether that's medication treatment, a good psychologically based treatment, or a validated bibliotherapy).

In another sense, the period "after" depression could benefit from special guidance. As we saw with Lonnie, the view from the other side of depression can be confusing and unfamiliar. This is a psychologically unique moment. Going through depression can change a person's self-understanding: What does it mean to have had depression? What does it mean to know that one is vulnerable to depression, even if depression is currently at bay? How should people bear (and think about) the weight of the past, even as they move through the present? Unfortunately, clinicians and researchers have not always given people the tools to work through these issues.

The period in the aftermath of depression also presents some unique opportunities. It is an ideal time to formulate a plan for your mood. It is a moment to take stock, to make sense of what happened in a mood episode, and to ensure you have all that is needed to manage mood going forward. Such an assessment may be done with a therapist or on your own. It's okay to be proud that you got well, just have the humility to admit that you can still learn more about your mood. No one—not even the experts—has perfect knowledge either of the sources of their own mood or of other people's moods.

Take stock of your mood in a comprehensive manner. Include the role of such things as how your mood might relate to

- your patterns of interaction with others;
- your thinking patterns;
- questionable life decisions;
- blocked or unrealistic goals;
- poor daily routines, particularly with respect to sleep, exercise, and light;
- major losses and stressors; and
- any hereditary vulnerability to depression and low mood.

It is a process. Your answers can change as you learn more. As you tally the contributions to your mood, don't expect a precise mathematical answer. Rough estimates are good enough.

The goal is simply to gain as much clarity as you can about the most important drivers of your mood.

Unfortunately, many squander this opportunity to take stock. Some people may avoid it because they hold a strongly biological view of depression: If depression is only a chemical imbalance, an accident of the brain, what more is there to plumb? By this logic, depression's causes are outside of human control and moving forward is only a matter of finding the right pharmaceutical. Others may experience depression as a time of pain and shame and do all they can to minimize backward glances. In such cases, analyzing what went wrong (or even what went well) amounts to "dwelling in the past" or opening a box that should stay closed.

Although sometimes uncomfortable, a "post battle assessment" of depression is worth the effort. Without one, you may not recognize how your own behaviors played into depression, or the critical changes you made in your life that helped to restore your mood. Indeed, taking stock may help you recognize key sources of your resilience, which you can draw upon to bolster mood during recovery. There are many different engines of positive mood, which can differ considerably from person to person. For one individual, it might be a regimen of physical exercise that is critical. For others, the key wellspring might be religious faith, involvement in the community, or devotion to a cause larger than oneself. For still others, the key wellspring of positive mood may be devotion to artistic pursuits or to a friend group. You have to discover which sources are most important for you.

Although we still don't know all the reasons why depression recurs for some and not for others, a careful post-battle assessment may be critical to breaking the cycle of depression. Psychotherapist Emmy Gut encapsulated these differences with a distinction between productive and unproductive depression, which speaks to how depression is ultimately processed (or not processed).

In unproductive depression, depression does not lead to learning or behavior change. The most tragic result is when people repeat the same self-destructive or self-defeating patterns in their lives, which can then play out over many episodes of depression. These patterns may include the following:

- Continuing to make risky life choices, such as repeated attraction to unreliable or even abusive romantic partners (with heartache and depression the inevitable results).
- Self-defeating ways of reacting to periods of low mood. For example, many people habitually turn to drugs or alcohol as a means to cope with stressful life periods—strategies that may feel good in the moment but feed depression over the long term.
- Remaining committed to failing life goals. Another potential trap is continuing to cling to an unrealistic life goal(s), despite evidence that the goal(s) will never be attained. Examples of such risky goals include becoming a reality TV star or supermodel, or even trying to win the affection of a rejecting parent.

By contrast, productive depression ushers in a better aftermath. Lonnie was like a poster child for the idea. She came to see clearly that her depression was a sign she needed to make major life changes. Most important, she came to understand that her goal of being a professional freelance writer was setting her, and her mood, up for failure. Opportunities in the writing career were few, and it was difficult to secure regular work, let alone advance. The writing task itself was isolating and did not offer Lonnie meaningful social interaction. As problematic, Lonnie saw how the rhythm of the writing work swallowed her in frequent downward spirals of mood: Periods of slow progress in writing would lead Lonnie to feel worse about herself; her mind would fill with negative self-reproach, which would make it more difficult to focus on the piece at hand. As deadlines came and went, her ability to work would degrade even further, her self-flagellation would increase, and her pit of depression would deepen.

Lonnie's depression was productive because it awakened her to an alternative life path. As her depression started to recede, she changed careers to social work. In a sense, Lonnie was "listening to her depression" in making this change. As a writer, she was isolated from people; social work could be a way to increase her level of connection to others. Lonnie also surmised that social work might be a way she could turn her terrible experience of depression into a force for good. In a sense, she even recast her personal struggles as a strength: These experiences increased her ability to empathize with patients who faced trying times, as well as her motivation to advocate for the most vulnerable. Finally, she recognized that her mood was worsened by the unstructured schedule of the writing life; this, too, could change with social work. As she joined an active practice and saw clients in regular hour long blocks, her workdays flew by. No, her new job was not perfect (for one, the pay and prestige could be higher), but for Lonnie it was the perfect fit.

What can be learned from depression?

Highlighting the possibility of productive depression should never be used to glamorize depression, trivialize the pain associated with mood disorders, or suggest that depression is somehow a good thing. But cases such as Lonnie, and there are many, dramatize the possibility that depression can offer people an opportunity to learn from the experience in important ways.

This learning is of course with the benefit of hindsight. In the thick of the episode, Lonnie could not imagine that her depression could contain any lessons. At the time, her life seemed like a total wreck. She was blocked in her career goals, withdrew from friends and family, and felt all alone in what seemed like a futile struggle. Her mind was not well—she could not think clearly, and when she did have thoughts, they came in a stream of negative recriminations. In the moment, her depression was a tornado, leaving only a debris field in its wake.

As we've seen, the final accounting was far more complex, in ways large and small. Seven years later, well into her recovery, Lonnie saw things differently. Obviously, she recognized ways her depression was destructive. As previously discussed, it led her to give up on her long-sought career as a freelance writer, which was a painful loss and blow to her self-esteem. At the same time, she also saw how her depression was creative. As highlighted, her new identification with the suffering led her to embark upon a new path as a social worker; her new job lent her life organization and purpose. As she stepped back, she saw other lessons, such as how depression may have taught her what true love was, which had blossomed into a marriage with Jonah. In a weird way, it may have even taught her what it meant to be a responsible adult.

There was still more. Despite turning her life upside down, Lonnie was able to identify several other unexpected things that she learned from her depression that still guide her to this day. Although her circumstances are of course unique, what she learned resonates with what is experienced by many depression sufferers:

Normal moods are precious. Before Lonnie got depressed, she was a typical moody teen. She was a perfectionistic. She would carry on when little things didn't go her way. It was natural to for her to sulk away an afternoon. After being violently buffeted by years of depression, Lonnie had a new reference point for mood. She also had a newfound appreciation for normal moods. After depression, she placed more value on just feeling okay. Good enough, even if not perfect, was good. She vowed to never take mental health for granted. In the same way that seeing a close friend go through a serious illness may give a person a new perspective on their minor ailments, Lonnie's trip through depression taught her to appreciate the fragility of mental health and to savor what of it that she had.

Learning empathy for others facing difficult times. Depression took nearly everything away from Lonnie. It stripped away her job, her boyfriend, her finances, and, obviously, her sense of equilibrium. Lonnie knew what it was like to be totally desperate, out of options, in need of help. She felt like the old Lonnie had lived a life of comfortable selfishness. As she got back on her feet, she wanted to pay it forward, to make amends. Her depression would have been worth it if she could devote herself to caring for others who were feeling similarly desperate and out of options. She returned to school for social work. She proved to be a model student; she became a case worker at the local hospital and then joined a private practice. It was a tough job, a job she loved, and a job she would never have found were it not for the depression. She would never wish depression on her worst enemy, yet she saw that depression might enable her to help others around her—not only strangers but also friends, co-workers, and family.

Seeing yourself as a survivor. Lonnie wanted to give up many, many times during her episodes. There were moments when her family likewise wanted to give up. But she never did. And neither did they. Weathering that most severe of storms and coming through is an important lesson—as Lonnie expected that life would someday throw another storm her way. Surviving depression—in her case, severe depression—was a kind of anchor and a sort of armor. She told herself, "If I can survive this, I can survive anything. Maybe it won't be pretty, but survive I will."

Life's minor irritations look more minor. Having survived the horror of depression, life's daily annoyances and hassles looked just a little bit smaller. In the past, Lonnie could get unglued by the annoying boss, the frustration of not being able to find a parking place in heavy traffic, the dog in the next apartment that wouldn't stop barking, or when her flight got canceled. Lonnie still didn't like being in these situations, but when she started to get wound up, she reminded herself how little these things were in comparison to her severe depression. It just usually didn't seem worth getting so upset anymore. With a broader perspective, minor annoyances no longer got under her skin.

Living life with a greater sense of purpose. When Lonnie was overwhelmed by depression, most elements of her life seemed senseless and random. Although she doesn't completely understand why depression turned her world upside down, the experience served as a huge wake-up call. Lonnie learned there were some parts of her life that needed work. Once her depression lifted, she seized the chance to work on those parts. Seared by the experience of chronic depression, she became a social worker and advocated for the less fortunate. After drifting through several relationships, she found Jonah and marriage. And with luck, she will become a mother before too much longer. Lonnie felt like she was being given second chances to make a difference. She vows that she will not waste them.

Lonnie's case has illustrated some of the ways that the aftermath of depression can foster new learning. Still, we cannot tie a bow neatly around this topic. Unfortunately, not every depression offers lessons, nor are depression's lessons the same for everyone. Like any complex human experience, there is no single takeaway. For some, depression might help them savor the simple pleasures of life; for others, it can serve as a means to find clarity in their core values; for still others, it may help them sort out who truly is there for them (and who is not). More systematic research is needed on what people learn from depression, including what clinicians can do to increase the chances that depression leads to positive life change.

Being prepared for relapse: Recommendations

Life after depression can be bright. But in addition to hoping for the best, it is important to plan for the worst. Despite all best efforts, low mood and depression may return. We end this chapter with five important recommendations for what to do when your mood spirals down:

1. Know your early warning signs. Everyone has some tells for when low mood or depression is creeping back into their life. It might be feeling fatigued or losing one's appetite. It might be losing the ability to concentrate or finding that everyday tasks such as laundry or doing the dishes take longer. Or it might be having less interest in work, school, or hanging out with friends. A key part of becoming a more educated consumer of your mood is learning to identify your warning signs. If you're not sure what these are, get feedback from a person who knows you well.

2. Know your mood triggers (and what you can do to mitigate them). When you are starting to struggle, be aware of situations that are most likely to worsen matters. It might be a demanding boss or work deadlines, or arguments with a spouse. Sometimes, it is possible to reduce your exposure to these triggers, for example, by reducing nonessential responsibilities or taking a break from a person who is causing you pain. Some triggers—such as a health problem or a change in the seasons—you have less control over. Here, you should focus on what you can do to minimize the impact. High on the list should be to allow yourself adequate time for rest and self-care. Remember that self-care is even more vital when you're dealing with a stressful situation.

3. Try not to panic or overreact. Instead, deploy the coping techniques that work best for you. It is hoped that you have taken advantage of your well period to build a good list of go-to practices or techniques. Whether that means getting extra sleep, venting your frustrations with a close confidant, or listening to a special music playlist, now is the moment to dig into your coping toolbox. If you have mindfulness

practices in your armory, know that regular deployment of these practices is among the best ways to defuse low mood and interrupt its escalation into more serious clinical depression.

4. Connect. One of the strongest impulses when low mood is returning is to withdraw from the world. Fight this urge. Make sure that you use your entire network of social support, whether online or face-to-face.

5. Have an action plan for what you will do if your initial steps are not successful and your mood worsens. This plan can be a formal document or it can be more informal. It is something you can develop with your loved ones or a treating professional, or you can develop it on your own. Your action plan should identify at what point you will act and whom you will call. If you are on the fence about seeking treatment, know that asking for help is not a sign of weakness—it is a sign that you understand depression and want to take action. There is no reason to wait until you are completely incapacitated by depression. Err on the side of action, as we know that getting help for depression earlier usually portends a better outcome.

16

CHARTING A NEW FUTURE FOR DEPRESSION

What are the biggest remaining myths about depression?

Public dialogue about depression and other mental health problems has taken small steps forward. It has become almost routine for well-known people such as actress Kristen Bell or comedian Maria Bamford to share their struggles with depression in great detail. One hopes that these disclosures help open up the conversation for others. For the average person, however, depression is still a tough subject, difficult to broach with friends, lovers, or employers. Often, when depression is discussed, it is discussed in hushed or apologetic tones. Progress in public attitudes toward mental health problems is more halting than we'd like. For example, recent survey data show one-third of Americans still report that "people with mental health disorders scare me."

Despite signs of progress, conversations about depression are often sidetracked or hijacked by widespread myths. Here, I detail some of the biggest fallacies about depression:

> *On some level, depressed people want to be depressed.* This myth is crystalized by the statement, "depression is a choice." A related misconception is the idea that depression could be erased by some small, easily accomplished step, such as "looking on the bright side," "going for a

walk," "just believing in yourself," or "trusting in god." What depressed person would not "snap out of it" if they could? If it were only so easy! The myth of choice does not endure because it is useful for the depressed person. It endures because it reduces the burden on those close to the depressed person. Blaming the depression on the actions (or the inactions) of a depressed person reduces the burden on others to help or even listen. Indeed, one could argue that the myth of choice fits into a larger cultural narrative around mental illness that allows governing bodies and institutions to absolve themselves of responsibility for mental health problems.

People with depression are weak. By this myth, depression reflects a weak will or a weak character. Of course, it's really the opposite. Depression requires extraordinary strength to withstand. During an episode, ordinary acts such as getting out of bed or showing up for work require an extra shot of fortitude. The myth of weakness is also convenient for bystanders. Viewing depressed people as deficient weaklings warrants them less sympathy and also suggests that helping them may not be the best use of time and energy. In addition to noting that the myth of weakness is hurtful, it is worth pointing out that many world historic figures have grappled with depression—a list of non-weaklings that among others includes Abraham Lincoln, Theodore Roosevelt, Winston Churchill, George Patton, Georgia O'Keefe, Sir Isaac Newton, Queen Victoria, and Charles Darwin.

Depressed people are "doing it for attention." This is wrong by any fair accounting. Most depressed people suffer in silence, concealing the true extent of their problems. A habit of concealing depression explains why depression receives too little clinical attention (and often too late). Why conceal? Because in this world, revelations of depression are still more likely to be penalized by friends, lovers, and employers than they are rewarded. Unfortunately, when depressed people do draw attention to their difficulties, others may minimize them or respond in other ineffective ways. Once again, the myth of "attention seeking" may endure because it gets other people off the hook. If depressed people are just broadcasting their symptoms for attention, there's little need to engage with the show. That would only "encourage them!"

Depression has a specific look or behavior. In this myth, the depressed person must follow a prescribed profile or be disqualified from depression. This includes disqualifications because "you don't look depressed," "I saw you laughing with your friends," or "you have a great life." The net effect of such statements is to negate or invalidate the depressed person's experience. Many depictions of depression in mass media feed this myth. Anyone who has read a news story about depression has likely seen the headclutcher—the stereotyped image of a pained, solitary figure sitting alone in a dimly lit room, holding their head with both arms. The headclutcher image replaces the confusing reality of depression with a cartoon. Such images belie the fact that there is no single type of depressed person, facial expression, or behavior. On the contrary, depression affects a wide swath of humanity in a variety of ways. In fact, unless you ask, there is no way to determine who is struggling with the condition and who is not.

Depression isn't real. The phrase, "It's all in your head" is a common form of this myth. This myth is sneaky. In one sense, yes, virtually every experience is in our heads: church bells ringing, the warmth of a comfortable blanket, the taste of a good Chianti. And it's also true that important aspects of depression come from inside our skull, from patterns of thinking to the brain's activity. Yet the idea of "all in your head" goes way too far. Depression also involves factors that are in the world. Whether it is exposure to trauma, grief, divorce, or job loss, important sources of depression are external to the person. Because environments matter, depression is never 100% "in your head." The idea is also harmful in another way. The "all in your head" concept would have us diminish the depressed person's psychological experience as a sort of illusion. We should never do that. The suffering is real, even if its source is mental.

Depression is just sadness. This myth may perpetuate itself because people are motivated to view depression in simplified easy-to-understand terms. Most everyone has felt sad, so it is tempting to make the leap that if you've experienced sadness, you must know what it feels like to have depression. This is a dangerous assumption. Equating clinical depression with garden-variety sadness both trivializes and oversimplifies clinical depression. As we've discussed, depression is both more serious and more complex than ordinary sadness. Some depressed people don't actually struggle with sadness. Sadness is very common, but it is not required for diagnosis. As you now know, depression covers a wide variety of symptoms (e.g., insomnia, weight loss, and concentration difficulties) and feeling states (e.g., guilt). Sadness may or may not be part of the package. Is a depressed person sad? If you are curious, the best way to learn what a person is going through is to ask them.

Although it is frustrating to see myths about depression continue, the maintaining forces behind these myths are strong. The concept of depression, like other mental conditions, is threatening. Like mortality, depression is an uncomfortable fact of the universe. Depression reminds us that we might not be in full control of our minds, that we might have vulnerability to mental health problems. Myths about depression may endure because they soothe such uncomfortable thoughts. When depressed people are viewed as foreign or as unworthy, it puts depression at a psychological distance. Likewise, viewing depressed people as losers who trump up their symptoms or who bring the problem on themselves gives other people permission to tune out the problem. However convenient that may be for the nondepressed person, these myths invariably harm depressed people, perpetuating stigma about the condition and leaving millions more isolated in their suffering.

What can the individual do to improve the conversation about depression?

Despite numerous public education campaigns, much work still needs to be done to correct public misconceptions about depression. Hearing friends or family repeat these misconceptions can be hurtful and discouraging. The good news is that everyone can do some simple things to improve the conversation. The more who participate, the more likely we are to achieve enduring change in how depression is viewed, with each small voice building to a larger chorus. We all have an obligation to debunk these myths.

If you have a personal connection to depression, having struggled with it yourself, or as a firsthand witness to a struggle of a close friend or family member, consider sharing your experience. (Note: If you are discussing another person's struggle, please first get permission.) Simple sharing is surprisingly powerful. Every time someone shares their depression experience, whether on social media, a blog, or in real life, it brings to light common threads that connect diverse individuals. Honest portrayals of depression have the power to erode stereotypes otherwise based in ignorance and fear. In addition, sharing models that it is okay to discuss the topic of depression, and each share may encourage others to come forward. Finally, if you share a story of recovery, it demonstrates that there is a real, tangible basis for healing and hope.

Another key step toward improving our public dialogue is actively learning about depression and mental health more broadly. For example, by reading this book (thanks! and don't forget the other readings I have recommended) and sharing what you discover, you can expand what your friends, family, or co-workers know about depression. Given widespread misunderstandings, there is value in sharing information about the causes of depression, its prevalence, how to talk about it, and how it can be treated. It is also a service to amplify reliable sources about mental health, including news stories, scientific articles, podcasts, or blog posts. Finally, public dialogue is served when you share resources concerning where others can turn for help with depression and related mental health problems, including online screening tools, hotlines, and support groups.

In this era of perpetual information overload, sometimes it is difficult to know what to believe. In building your knowledge of depression and mental health, search for vetted sources. Vetted sources include news outlets that have dedicated science coverage, established research scientists, and work that is published in peer-reviewed journals (see Resources for examples of reliable mental health sources). Caveat emptor! Be careful of information, treatments, or solutions that seem "too good to be true (3 easy steps to cure depression)" or that are intended to sell you something (a device or product).

It can be particularly challenging to create dialogue about mental health during everyday conversations. Some people are not open to listening to new perspectives. Many moments (e.g., during a funeral service) are not appropriate to try to change minds about mental health. And such conversations can also get tangled in politics, which is its own thicket. You have to pick your spots carefully. For example, imagine you are talking to your friend, and your friend comments on someone in your circle, Pat, who you both know is struggling with depression after a breakup. After a recent conversation with Pat, your friend says, "All she does is talk in circles and feel sorry for herself. She's become such a downer. I don't know why she can't just get over it." This moment is a perfect time to gently step in as an advocate for Pat to correct your friend, saying something along the lines of "I hear what you're saying. You know, depression can be really frustrating for everyone, so let's take turns supporting her. I know Pat doesn't mean to be a downer; she's just going through a hard time now."

Finally, you can have conversations directly with a person who is struggling. In these settings, you may provide information, reassurance, or advocacy. For example, many people who struggle with depression are unaware of the kinds of treatments that are available. Advocates can use one-on-one mental health conversations to help a depressed person become more empowered and knowledgeable about depression. One-on-one conversations are a way to link people who are struggling to mental health services or to help them feel more supported in their health care decisions. Sometimes, the most powerful thing in direct conversation is to say nothing and simply provide a listening ear, especially during moments of crisis or frustration.

How can the individual help bring about broader social changes that reduce the toll of depression?

We end with a paradox. Many Western societies place a paramount importance on the pursuit of happiness. In the United States, happiness is enshrined as an inalienable right. At the same time, depression is at epidemic levels in many countries throughout the world. The strangest thing of all is that happiness can be valued so highly as an individual good yet we accept skyrocketing rates of depression in the population as normal or expected. Virtually every week, yet another set of dire statistics on depression, anxiety, and suicide is reported and seems to be received with what amounts to a collective shrug. In recent years, this situation has been further inflamed by the COVID-19 pandemic. Awareness of depression certainly has grown during the pandemic as feelings of depression and anxiety become almost the norm for many citizens. Yet we still don't see a full public mobilization on the issue of mental health. In the United States, the public tolerates 45,000 deaths by suicide a year (many of them fueled by depression). One could argue that these deaths are accepted in a way that would never be accepted from other causes. Imagine the outcry if a 737 jet crashed every day?

How can we move to a world not only in which depression is discussed openly but also in which we begin to reduce this toll? What will it take to get adequate amounts of research or effective depression treatments that are widely available and accessible? Is it even realistic to dream of a future in which depression prevention is taken seriously?

This is a major agenda. The following are some key things the individual can do:

1. It bears reiterating that central to this effort is talking about depression in an open and honest way. A more open dialogue is a key to marshalling others to action and affecting broader social change. One might ask why events such as car washes, golf tournaments, or dance marathons are still not held to raise awareness of and funding for depression, whereas they are routinely held for breast cancer. Contrasting depression and cancer is apt because cancer was previously an "unspeakable" topic much like depression. But now cancer has become fully speakable. As breast cancer advocates found ways to break through taboos, other people became proud to talk about it (as survivors or supporters), donate money to the cause, and become active in support organizations. How will we bring depression to the same point? A reasonable hypothesis is that efforts to open up the conversation about depression will be repaid with more accepting attitudes, increased funding, and more supportive public policy.

2. The individual can also affect change in the domain of politics. In the clamor of public life, mental health causes can often get drowned out. Ask candidates for local, state, and national office about their mental health agenda. Vote for candidates who encourage government to spend more on prediction and prevention and devote appropriate resources to depression and other serious mental conditions.

Perhaps, even consider running for a leadership position yourself to raise the profile of mental health issues.

3. If you want to be involved in advocating for depressed people, volunteering your time for a mental health organization is a good option. Joining a local chapter of organizations such as the National Alliance for Mental Illness is a way to directly engage with your local community and be visible as a mental health ally. Increasingly, there are also opportunities to receive training to become involved in peer support programs. Among these are Mental Health First Aid programs, which are brief courses (often for no or low cost) that teach people how to help someone who may be experiencing a mental health or substance use challenge, including instruction on how to identify, understand, and respond to signs of various mental health problems.

4. George Bernard Shaw was quoted as saying that "a lack of money is the root of all evil." Although this may be an overstatement, mental health causes are chronically underfunded, especially given the scale of the problem. Thus, an important set of actions is financial, donating money to mental health causes if you have the means or fundraising on behalf of an organization that contributes to depression research, depression treatment, or depression prevention.

Is there really reason for hope?

These are the last words of the book, and I am writing in a dark time during which depression is running rampant across most Western societies.

I am hopeful about the future of depression, with caveats.

First, we will never reduce depression to zero. Depression is a capability built into our species over millions of years of evolution. Knowing this is to know that it is, in a sense, normal, to be depressed when one is facing things such as a health crisis, political disunity, poor economic prospects, or all of these at once. Zero depression is not the goal. Still, so much remains that could be done to contain the toll that depression takes—so that bouts of depression are shorter and less crippling and that people can experience periods of depression without feeling shame or like they are crazy or freaks. And, when all else fails and a severe depression strikes, we give people more tools to overcome it and absorb its lessons to enable a better life after depression. We cannot change our capability for depression; we can only change how we respond to it as individuals and as a society. Progress on both fronts is ultimately needed to contain depression.

Second, because depression will be a formidable problem for the foreseeable future, we need all hands on deck. This book was written by a psychologist and obviously features a psychological analysis of depression, including accounts of what causes it, how to treat it, and what we can do to foster change in the broader dialogue about this misunderstood condition. I stand behind this analysis of what psychology can contribute to. However, we must bring everything to bear on depression if we are to move the needle. This includes ordinary concerned citizens taking action in the ways outlined previously. And it includes experts in other disciplines who can come at depression from unique angles, including economics (Can markets be regulated in ways that raise human happiness?), communications (What messages and strategies can be deployed to change attitudes about depression?), sociology (How can key institutions and social structures be reformed to reduce depression?), and even architecture and urban planning (Can improving the built environment, traffic, or parks alleviate depression?). Finally, we need the skill of people from policy and administration to assemble all these experts and to synthesize their knowledge.

In a dark time, hope for the future is a challenging posture but also a realistic one—if we work together.

RESOURCES

Recommended Books: General Depression

Bonnano, G. A. (2009). *The other side of sadness: What the new science of bereavement tells us about life after loss*. Basic Books.

Casey, N. (Ed.). (2002). *Unholy ghost: Writers on depression*. Perennial.

Ghaemi, N. (2013). *On depression: Drugs, diagnosis, and despair in the modern world*. Johns Hopkins University Press.

Gotlib, I. H., & Hammen, C. L. (Eds.). (2015). *Handbook of depression* (3rd ed.). Guilford.

Greenberg, G. (2010). *Manufacturing depression. The secret history of a modern disease*. Simon & Schuster.

Haig, M. (2015). *Reasons to stay alive*. Penguin.

Harri, J. (2019). *Lost connections: Why you're depressed and how to find hope*. Bloomsbury.

Horwitz, A. V., & Wakefield, J. C. (2007). *The loss of sadness: How psychiatry transformed normal sorrow into depressive disorder*. Oxford University Press.

Kramer, P. D. (2006). *Against depression*. Penguin.

Merkin, D. (2017). *This close to happy: A reckoning with depression*. Farrar, Straus & Giroux.

Nesse, R. M. (2020). *Good reasons for bad feelings: Insights from the frontier of evolutionary psychiatry*. Penguin.

Rottenberg, J. (2014). *The depths: The evolutionary origins of the depression epidemic*. Basic Books.

Salomon, A. (2002). *The noonday demon: An atlas of depression*. Scribner.

Styron, W. (1990). *Darkness visible: A memoir of madness*. Vintage.

Recommended Books: Bipolar Disorder

Fawcet, J., Golden, B., & Rosenfeld, N. (2007). *New hope for people with bipolar disorder: Your friendly, authoritative guide to the latest in traditional and complementary solutions* (2nd ed.). Three Rivers Press.

Jamison, K. R. (1993). *Touched with fire: Manic-depressive illness and the artistic temperament.* Free Press.

Jamison, K. R. (1995). *An unquiet mind: A memoir of moods and madness.* Knopf.

Miklowitz, D. J. (2010). *The bipolar disorder survival guide: What you and your family need to know* (3rd ed.). Guilford.

Mondimore, F. M. (2014). *Bipolar disorder: A guide for patients and families* (3rd ed.). Johns Hopkins University Press.

Recommended Self-Help Books

Burns, D. D. (1999). *Feeling good: The new mood therapy.* HarperCollins.

Edelman, S. (2007). *Change your thinking: Overcome stress, anxiety, and depression, and improve your life with CBT.* Marlow.

Greenberger, D., & Padesky, C. (1995). *Mind over mood: Change how you feel by changing the way you think.* Guilford.

Harris, R. (2008). *The happiness trap: How to stop struggling and start living.* Shambala.

Illardi, S. S. (2009). *The depression cure: The 6-step program to beat depression without drugs.* Da Capo Press.

Lewinsohn, P. (1992). *Control your depression.* Fireside.

Maisel, E. (2012). *Rethinking depression: How to shed mental health labels and create personal meaning.* New World Library.

Parker, G. (2004). *Dealing with depression.* Allen & Unwin.

Tanner, S., & Ball, J. (2000). *Beating the blues: A self-help approach to overcoming depression.* Doubleday.

Teasdale, J. D., & Segal, Z. V. (2007). *The mindful way through depression: Freeing yourself from chronic unhappiness.* Guilford.

Thase, M. E., & Lang, S. S. (2006). *Beating the blues: New approaches to overcoming dysthymia and chronic mild depression.* Oxford University Press.

Recommended Internet Therapy Websites

Beating the Blues: http://www.beatingtheblues.co.uk
eCouch: https://ecouch.anu.edu.au/welcome
Good Days Ahead: https://www.gooddaysahead.com/about
Mental Health Online: https://www.mentalhealthonline.org.au

MoodGYM: https://moodgym.anu.edu.au/welcome

This Way Up: https://thiswayup.org.au

Internet Resources for Crisis Management

American Foundation for Suicide Prevention, suicide warning signs: https://adaa.org/learn-from-us/from-the-experts/blog-posts/suicide-warning-signs

American Foundation for Suicide Prevention, supporting an at-risk person: https://afsp.org/find-support/when-someone-is-at-risk

Herefordshire and Worcestershire Health and Care NHS Trust, tips for good communication: https://www.hacw.nhs.uk/our-services/patient-selfmanagement/communication

National Alliance on Mental Illness, Calling 911 and talking with the police: http://www.nami.org/Find-Support/Family-Members-and-Caregivers/Calling-911-and-Talking-with-the-Police

Wikipedia, global helpline and suicide hotline links: https://en.wikipedia.org/wiki/List_of_suicide_crisis_lines

Reliable News and Information Sources for Citizens to Learn More About Depression

BBC News

The Conversation

The Guardian

National Institute of Mental Health

National Public Radio

Nature News

New Scientist

The New York Times

ScienceThe Washington Post

Wired

Key Peer-Reviewed Journals That Publish on Depression in the Fields of Psychology, Psychiatry, and Public Health

American Journal of Psychiatry

British Journal of Psychiatry

Clinical Psychology Review

Clinical Psychology: Science and Practice

JAMA: Psychiatry

Journal of Abnormal Psychology

Journal of Affective Disorders
Journal of Consulting and Clinical Psychology
Lancet
New England Journal of Medicine
Psychological Clinical Science

INDEX

For the benefit of digital users, indexed terms that span two pages (e.g., 52–53) may, on occasion, appear on only one of those pages.